WORD by WORD

BASIC

DICCIONARIO ILUSTRADO DE INGLÉS

English/Spanish Picture Dictionary

Steven J. Molinsky · Bill Bliss

Herlinda Charpentier Saitz

Longman

Library of Congress Cataloging-in-Publication Data

Molinsky, Steven J.
   Word by word picture dictionary / Steven J. Molinsky, Bill Bliss.
      p.   cm.
   Abridged version of Word by word picture dictionary.
   Includes index.
   ISBN 0-13-278573-0 (paper) : 8.00
   1. Picture dictionaries, English 2. English language—Textbooks for foreign speakers.
I. Bliss, Bill.   II. Molinsky, Steven J.   Word by word picture dictionary.   III. Title.
PE1629.M582   1995   423'.1—dc20   95-717 CIP

Publisher: *Louisa B. Hellegers*
Development Editor: *Carol Callahan*
Production Editor: *Kelly A. Tavares*
Art Director: *Merle Krumper*
Manufacturing Manager: *Ray Keating*

Illustrated by RICHARD E. HILL

The authors gratefully acknowledge the contribution of Tina Carver
in the development of the *Word by Word* program.

© 1997 by Prentice Hall Regents
A Pearson Education Company
Pearson Education, 10 Bank Street, White Plains, NY 10606

Printed in the United States of America
10   9   8

ISBN 0-13-278573-0

ÍNDICE/CONTENIDO CONTENTS iii

El diccionario ilustrado *Word by Word Basic* contiene más de 1.500 palabras con ilustraciones de colores vívidos y ofrece el vocabulario esencial necesario para comunicarse efectivamente en una amplia variedad de situaciones y contextos. Este texto es una versión reducida del diccionario ilustrado *Word by Word* de 3.000 palabras.

Word by Word Basic organiza cuidadosamente el vocabulario en 67 unidades temáticas con una secuencia de lecciones cuyos temas abarcan desde las experiencias más inmediatas al estudiante hasta aquellas pertinentes al mundo que lo rodea. A las primeras unidades, dedicadas a la familia, la casa, los hábitos y quehaceres domésticos, siguen lecciones sobre la comunidad, la escuela, el trabajo, como ir de compras, y otras. *Word by Word Basic* ofrece el vocabulario esencial para sobrevivir tanto en las faenas de la vida diaria como en las actividades escolares fuera o dentro del ámbito escolar. *Word by Word Basic* puede emplearse en la secuencia en que aparecen los temas o en cualquier otro orden que se desee.

Para mayor conveniencia en el manejo del manual las listas de referencia de los títulos de las unidades se han presentado de dos maneras: en el Contenido aparecen tal como se presentan en el texto y en el Índice temático, en orden alfabético. Esta presentación junto con el Glosario en el apéndice permite que tanto los estudiantes como los profesores puedan localizar fácil y rápidamente todas las palabras y los temas del diccionario.

El diccionario ilustrado *Word by Word Basic* es el texto central del *Programa completo de desarrollo de vocabulario básico* que comprende una extensa selección de materiales impresos y audiovisuales para la instrucción del inglés en los niveles básicos.

Los materiales auxiliares incluyen cuadernos de ejercicios en dos niveles (básico y de alfabetización), un manual con estrategias para la enseñanza, un programa completo de audiocintas, láminas, diaspositivas a colores, un juego de vocabulario en tarjetas, un álbum de canciones con su propio libro y un programa de ejercicios de evaluación. El diccionario ilustrado *Word by Word Básico* también ofrece ediciones bilingües.

Estrategias Didácticas

Word by Word Basic presenta el vocabulario dentro de un contexto. Las palabras se usan en conversaciones modelo que reproducen con fidelidad su uso acostumbrado. Los modelos sirven de base para que los estudiantes se entreguen a prácticas de conversación interactivas y dinámicas. Además, en cada unidad hay preguntas de discusión y redacción para estimularlos a relacionar el vocabulario y los temas a sus propias vidas mientras comparten experiencias, pensamientos, opiniones e información sobre sí mismos, su cultura y sus países. De esta forma, los estudiantes llegan a conocerse "palabra por palabra".

Al usar *Word by Word Basic* los animamos a desarrollar estrategias que sean compatibles con su propio estilo de enseñanza y las necesidades y habilidades de sus estudiantes. Para presentar y practicar el vocabulario de cada unidad puede ser útil incorporar algunas de las siguientes técnicas.

1. *Preparación del vocabulario:* estimule el conocimiento previo del vocabulario que tengan los alumnos, ya sea provocándolos a que usen las palabras en la unidad que ellos ya conocen, escribiendo dichas palabras en la pizarra o haciendo que miren las láminas, las diapositivas o las ilustraciones de *Word by Word Basic,* e identifiquen aquellas con las que están familiarizados.

2. *Presentación del vocabulario:* señale la ilustración de cada palabra, repitiéndola en voz alta y haciendo que los alumnos la repitan en coro e individualmente. Tenga presente la necesidad de verificar la comprensión y pronunciación del vocabulario.

3. *Práctica del vocabulario:* haga que los alumnos practiquen el vocabulario en clase como grupo, en parejas o en grupos pequeños. Pronuncie o escriba una palabra y haga que los alumnos señalen la ilustración o digan el número correspondiente a la misma; o señale una ilustración o diga el número y haga que los alumnos pronuncien la palabra a que éste pertenece.

4. *Práctica de conversaciones modelo:* algunas unidades contienen conversaciones modelo que usan la primera palabra en la lista del vocabulario. Otras conversaciones modelo están en forma de diálogos esquemáticos en que se pueden insertar las palabras del vocabulario. En muchos diálogos esquemáticos hay números en corchetes que indican cuáles palabras pueden usarse para practicar la conversación. Si no aparecen números en corchetes, se pueden utilizar todas las palabras en la página.

Se recomiendan los siguientes pasos para la práctica de conversaciones modelo:

a. Presentación: los alumnos observan la ilustración e intercambian ideas sobre quiénes serán los que hablan y dónde tiene lugar la conversación.

b. Se presenta y se verifica la comprensión de la situación y del vocabulario.

c. Los alumnos repiten cada línea de la conversación en coro o individualmente.

d. Los alumnos practican el modelo en parejas.

e. Una pareja de estudiantes presenta la conversación nueva basada en el modelo, usando diferentes palabras del vocabulario.

f. Basándose en el modelo los alumnos, en parejas, practican varias conversaciones nuevas usando diferentes palabras del vocabulario.

g. Cada pareja presenta su diálogo al resto de la clase.

5. *Práctica de escritura y ortografía:* haga que los alumnos practiquen deletreando las palabras en clase, como grupo, en pares o en grupos pequeños. Diga o deletree una palabra y luego haga que los alumnos la escriban y señalen la ilustración o el número que le corresponde. O, señale una ilustración o diga un número; luego haga que los alumnos escriban la palabra.

6. *Temas para discusión, composición, diarios y archivos:* todas las unidades en *Word by Word Basic* suministran una o más preguntas que pueden servir para discutir o para escribir sobre el tema de la unidad. Éstas se encuentran en áreas sombreadas de verde al pie de la página. Haga que los alumnos respondan a las preguntas en clase, en pares o en grupos pequeños; o haga que los alumnos escriban sus respuestas en casa, comparen su trabajo con otros compañeros y lo discutan en clase con sus compañeros, ya sea en pares o en grupos pequeños.

Los alumnos pueden interesarse en llevar un diario de su trabajo escrito. Si lo permite el tiempo, usted puede contestarle a cada uno, por escrito, compartiendo sus opiniones y experiencias o reaccionando a lo que ellos hayan escrito. Si usted archiva el trabajo escrito de sus alumnos, estas composiciones son un excelente testimonio de su progreso y aprendizaje del inglés.

7. *Actividades comunicativas:* la guía didáctica provee innumerables maneras para estimular y provocar a los alumnos con la intención de aprovechar los diferentes estilos, preferencias y habilidades particulares que los ayuden en su aprendizaje. Entre ellos, juegos, proyectos, discusiones, movimientos, dibujos, pantomimas y dramatizaciones. Escoja, en cada unidad, una o más actividades para afianzar el aprendizaje del vocabulario, de manera que haga del mismo una experiencia estimulante, creativa y placentera.

Word by Word Basic intenta ofrecerles a los estudiantes una manera vívida y significativa de practicar el vocabulario inglés. Al expresarle el fin de nuestro programa, esperamos haberle comunicado también su esencia: aprender vocabulario puede estimular una interacción auténtica . . . puede relacionarse a la experiencia personal de los alumnos . . . puede ser pertinente a las diferentes habilidades y estilos de aprendizaje de ellos, y . . . ¡puede ser divertido!

Steven J. Molinsky
Bill Bliss

The *Word by Word Basic Picture Dictionary* presents over 1500 vocabulary words through lively full-color illustrations. This innovative Picture Dictionary offers students at the low-beginning and literacy levels of English the essential vocabulary they need for everyday language and survival needs. This text is an abridged version of the "full" *Word by Word Picture Dictionary.*

Word by Word Basic organizes the vocabulary into 67 thematic units, providing a careful sequence of lessons that range from the immediate world of the student to the world at large. Early units on the family, the home, and daily activities lead to lessons on the community, school, work-place, shopping, and other topics. *Word by Word Basic* provides coverage of important lifeskill competencies and the vocabulary of school subjects and extracurricular activities. Since each unit is self-contained, *Word by Word Basic* can be used either sequentially or in any desired order.

For users' convenience, the units of *Word by Word Basic* are listed in two ways: sequentially in the Table of Contents, and alphabetically in the Thematic Index. These resources, combined with the Glossary in the appendix, allow students and teachers to easily locate all words and topics in the Picture Dictionary.

The *Word by Word Basic Picture Dictionary* is the centerpiece of the complete *Word by Word Basic Vocabulary Development Program*, which offers a wide selection of print and media support materials for instruction at the low-beginning and literacy levels. Ancillary materials include Beginning and Literacy level Workbooks, a Teacher's Resource Book, a complete Audio Program, Wall Charts, Color Transparencies, Vocabulary Game Cards, a Song Album and accompanying Songbook, and a Testing Program. Bilingual editions of the Basic Picture Dictionary are also available.

Teaching Strategies

Word by Word Basic presents vocabulary words in context. Model conversations depict situations in which people use the words in meaningful communication. These models become the basis for students to engage in dynamic, interactive conversational practice. In addition, writing and discussion questions in each unit encourage students to relate the vocabulary and themes to their own lives as they share experiences, thoughts, opinions, and information about themselves, their cultures, and their countries. In this way, students get to know each other "word by word."

In using *Word by Word Basic*, we encourage you to develop approaches and strategies that are compatible with your own teaching style and the needs and abilities of your students. You may find it helpful to incorporate some of the following techniques for presenting and practicing the vocabulary in each unit.

1. *Previewing the Vocabulary:* Activate students' prior knowledge of the vocabulary either by brainstorming with students the words in the unit they already know and writing them on the board, or by having students look at the Wall Chart, the transparency, or the illustration in *Word by Word* and identify the words they are familiar with.

2. *Presenting the Vocabulary:* Point to the picture of each word, say the word, and have the class repeat it chorally and individually. Check students' understanding and pronunciation of the vocabulary.

3. *Vocabulary Practice:* Have students practice the vocabulary as a class, in pairs, or in small groups. Say or write a word, and have students point to the item or tell the number. Or, point to an item or give the number, and have students say the word.

4. *Model Conversation Practice:* Some units have model conversations that use the first word in the vocabulary list. Other models are in the form of *skeletal dialogs*, in which vocabulary words can be inserted. (In many skeletal dialogs, bracketed numbers indicate which words can be used to practice the conversation. If no bracketed numbers appear, all the words on the page can be used.)

The following steps are recommended for Model Conversation Practice:

a. Preview: Students look at the model illustration and discuss who they think the speakers are and where the conversation takes place.

b. The teacher presents the model and checks students' understanding of the situation and the vocabulary.

c. Students repeat each line of the conversation chorally or individually.

d. Students practice the model in pairs.

e. A pair of students presents a new conversation based on the model, but using a different word from the vocabulary list.

f. In pairs, students practice several new conversations based on the model, using different vocabulary words.

g. Pairs present their conversations to the class.

5. *Writing and Spelling Practice:* Have students practice spelling the words as a class, in pairs, or in small groups. Say or spell a word, and have students write it and then point to the picture of the item or tell the number. Or, point to a picture of an item or give the number, and have students write the word.

6. *Themes for Discussion, Composition, Journals, and Portfolios:* Each unit of *Word by Word* provides one or more questions for discussion and composition. (These can be found in a green-shaded area at the bottom of the page.) Have students respond to the questions as a class, in pairs, or in small groups. Or, have students write their responses at home, share their written work with other students, and discuss as a class, in pairs, or in small groups.

Students may enjoy keeping a journal of their written work. If time permits, you may want to write a response in each student's journal, sharing your own opinions and experiences as well as reacting to what the student has written. If you are keeping portfolios of students'

work, these compositions serve as excellent examples of students' progress in learning English.

7. *Communication Activities:* The *Word by Word Basic* Teacher's Resource Book provides a wealth of games, tasks, brainstorming, discussion, movement, drawing, miming, role-playing, and other activities designed to take advantage of students' different learning styles and particular abilities and strengths. For each unit, choose one or more of these activities to reinforce students' vocabulary learning in a way that is stimulating, creative, and enjoyable.

Word by Word Basic aims to offer students a communicative, meaningful, and lively way of practicing English vocabulary. In conveying to you the substance of our program, we hope that we have also conveyed the spirit: that learning vocabulary can be genuinely interactive . . . relevant to our students' lives . . . responsive to students' differing strengths and learning styles . . . and fun!

Steven J. Molinsky
Bill Bliss

WORD by WORD

BASIC

DICCIONARIO ILUSTRADO DE INGLÉS

English/Spanish Picture Dictionary

Steven J. Molinsky · Bill Bliss

Herlinda Charpentier Saitz

nombre completo	**1.**	name
nombre(s)	**2.**	first name
otro(s) nombre(s)/segundo nombre	**3.**	middle name
apellidos (paterno y materno)	**4.**	last name
dirección	**5.**	address
número de la casa	**6.**	street number
calle	**7.**	street
número del apartamento	**8.**	apartment number
ciudad	**9.**	city
estado	**10.**	state
código/zona postal	**11.**	zip code
código telefónico/prefijo telefónico/ clave telefónica	**12.**	area code
número de teléfono	**13.**	telephone number/phone number
número de seguro social	**14.**	social security number

A. What's your **name**?
B. *Nancy Ann Peterson.*

Tell about yourself:
    My name is …………
    My address is …………
    My telephone number is …………
Now interview a friend.

esposa	**1.** wife	**hijos**	**children**	**abuelos**	**grandparents**
esposo	**2.** husband	hija	**5.** daughter	abuela	**10.** grandmother
		hijo	**6.** son	abuelo	**11.** grandfather
padres	**parents**	hermana	**7.** sister		
madre/mamá	**3.** mother	hermano	**8.** brother	**nietos**	**grandchildren**
padre/papá	**4.** father	bebé/nene/nena	**9.** baby	nieta	**12.** granddaughter
				nieto	**13.** grandson

A. Who is she?
B. She's my **wife**.
A. What's her name?
B. Her name is *Betty*.

A. Who is he?
B. He's my **husband**.
A. What's his name?
B. His name is *Fred*.

Tell about your family.
Talk about photos of family members.

tía	**1.** aunt	suegra	**6.** mother-in-law
tío	**2.** uncle	suegro	**7.** father-in-law
sobrina	**3.** niece	yerno	**8.** son-in-law
sobrino	**4.** nephew	nuera	**9.** daughter-in-law
primo, prima	**5.** cousin	cuñado	**10.** brother-in-law
		cuñada	**11.** sister-in-law

A. Who is she?
B. She's my **aunt**.
A. What's her name?
B. Her name is *Linda*.

A. Who is he?
B. He's my **uncle**.
A. What's his name?
B. His name is *Jack*.

Tell about your relatives:
   What are their names?
   Where do they live?
Draw your family tree and talk
   about it.

levantarse	**1.** get up		bañarse	**13.** take a bath
ducharse	**2.** take a shower		acostarse	**14.** go to bed
lavarme los dientes	**3.** brush *my** teeth		dormir	**15.** sleep
usar la seda/el hilo dental	**4.** floss *my** teeth		hacer/ preparar el desayuno	**16.** make breakfast
afeitarse	**5.** shave			
vestirse	**6.** get dressed		hacer/ preparar el almuerzo	**17.** make lunch
lavarme la cara	**7.** wash *my** face			
maquillarse/pintarse	**8.** put on makeup		hacer/ preparar la cena	**18.** cook/make dinner
cepillarse el cabello	**9.** brush *my** hair			
peinarse el cabello	**10.** comb *my** hair		desayunar	**19.** eat/have breakfast
hacer la cama	**11.** make the bed		comer/almorzar	**20.** eat/have lunch
desvestirse	**12.** get undressed		comer/cenar	**21.** eat/have dinner

* my, his, her, our, your, their

A. What do you do every day?

B. I **get up**, I **take a shower**, and I **brush my teeth**.

What do you do every day?
   Make a list.
Interview some friends and tell about their everyday activities.

limpiar el apartamento/ limpiar la casa	**1.** clean the apartment/ clean the house	escuchar/oír el radio	**12.** listen to the radio
barrer	**2.** sweep the floor	escuchar/oír música	**13.** listen to music
sacudir	**3.** dust	leer	**14.** read
pasar la aspiradora	**4.** vacuum	jugar	**15.** play
lavar los platos	**5.** wash the dishes	jugar baloncesto/ básquetbol	**16.** play basketball
lavar la ropa	**6.** do the laundry		
planchar	**7.** iron	tocar la guitarra	**17.** play the guitar
darle de comer al bebé/ al nene/a la nena	**8.** feed the baby	practicar el piano	**18.** practice the piano
		estudiar	**19.** study
darle de comer al gato	**9.** feed the cat	hacer ejercicios	**20.** exercise
pasear al perro	**10.** walk the dog		
ver/mirar la televisión/ la tele/el televisor	**11.** watch TV		

A. Hi! What are you doing?
B. I'm **clean**ing **the apartment**.

What are you going to do tomorrow?
(Tomorrow I'm going to
_____, _____,
_____, ...)

maestro(a)	1.	teacher
asistente/auxiliar	2.	teacher's aide
alumno/estudiante	3.	student
banco/silla	4.	seat/chair
pluma/bolígrafo	5.	pen
lápiz	6.	pencil
borrador/goma de borrar	7.	eraser
pupitre/escritorio	8.	desk
escritorio de la maestra	9.	teacher's desk
libro/libro de texto	10.	book/textbook
cuaderno/libreta	11.	notebook
papel	12.	notebook paper
papel cuadriculado	13.	graph paper
regla	14.	ruler
calculadora	15.	calculator
reloj	16.	clock
bandera	17.	flag
pizarra/pizarrón/tablero	18.	board
tiza/gis/pizarrín	19.	chalk
repisa	20.	chalk tray
borrador	21.	eraser
sistema de altavoz/altoparlante	22.	P.A. system/loudspeaker
cartelera/tablero/tabilla/mural de anuncios	23.	bulletin board
tachuela	24.	thumbtack
mapa	25.	map
sacapuntas	26.	pencil sharpener
globo terráqueo/del mundo	27.	globe
librera/librero/estante para libros	28.	bookshelf
retroproyector	29.	overhead projector
televisor/tele	30.	TV
pantalla	31.	(movie) screen
proyector de diapositivas/de transparencias	32.	slide projector
computadora	33.	computer
proyector de películas	34.	(movie) projector

A. Where's the **teacher**?
B. The **teacher** is *next to* the **board**.

A. Where's the **pen**?
B. The **pen** is *on* the **desk**.

Describe your classroom.
(There's a/an ....)

Levánte(n)se.	**1.** Stand up.
Vaya(n) *al pizarrón/ a la pizarra/al tablero.*	**2.** Go to the *board.*
Escriba(n) *su nombre.*	**3.** Write *your name.*
Borre(n) *su nombre.*	**4.** Erase *your name.*
Siénte(n)se/Tome(n) *asiento.*	**5.** Sit down./ Take your seat.
Abra(n) *el libro.*	**6.** Open *your book.*
Lea(n) *la página ocho.*	**7.** Read *page eight.*
Estudie(n) *la página ocho.*	**8.** Study *page eight.*
Cierre(n) *el libro.*	**9.** Close *your book.*
Guarde(n) *el libro.*	**10.** Put away *your book.*
Escuche(n) *la pregunta.*	**11.** Listen to *the question.*
Alce(n)/Levante(n) *la mano.*	**12.** Raise *your hand.*
Conteste(n) *la pregunta.*	**13.** Give *the answer.*
Trabaje(n) *en grupos.*	**14.** Work *in groups.*
Ayúdense.	**15.** Help *each other.*

Practice these classroom actions.

You're the teacher!
Give instructions to your students.

Haga(n) *su tarea.* **1.** Do *your homework.*

Traiga(n) *su tarea.* **2.** Bring in *your homework.*

Revise(n) *las respuestas/* **3.** Go over *the answers.*
las contestaciones.

Corrija(n) *sus errores.* **4.** Correct *your mistakes.*

Entregue(n) *su tarea.* **5.** Hand in *your homework.*

Saque(n) *un papel.* **6.** Take out *a piece of paper.*

Pase(n) *el examen/la prueba.* **7.** Pass out *the tests.*

Conteste(n) *las preguntas.* **8.** Answer *the questions.*

Revise(n) *sus respuestas/* **9.** Check *your answers.*
sus contestaciones.

Recoja(n) *los exámenes/* **10.** Collect *the tests.*
las pruebas.

Baje(n) *las persianas.* **11.** Lower *the shades.*

Apague(n) *las luces.* **12.** Turn off *the lights.*

Prenda(n)/Ponga(n)/ **13.** Turn on *the projector.*
Enciendan *el proyector.*

Vea(n) *la película.* **14.** Watch *the movie.*

Tome(n)/apuentes *notas.* **15.** Take notes.

Practice these classroom actions.

You're the teacher!
Give instructions to your students.

edificio de apartamentos	**1.** apartment (building)
casa	**2.** (single-family) house
duplex/casas de dos plantas/adosadas en pares	**3.** duplex/two-family house
casas en hileras/de dos o tres plantas en hileras	**4.** townhouse/townhome
condominio/condo/piso	**5.** condominium/condo
dormitorio/residencia estudiantil	**6.** dormitory/dorm
caraván/casa móvil/casa rodante/trailer	**7.** mobile home/trailer
hacienda/granja/finca	**8.** farmhouse
cabaña	**9.** cabin
asilo/casa de ancianos/de reposo/ para personas de la tercera edad	**10.** nursing home
refugio/albergue/asilo para pobres	**11.** shelter
casa flotante	**12.** houseboat

A. Where do you live?
B. I live in an **apartment building**.

Tell about people you know
   and the types of housing
   they live in.
Discuss:
   Who lives in dormitories?
   Who lives in nursing homes?
   Who lives in shelters?
   Why?

mesa de centro	**1.**	coffee table
alfombra	**2.**	rug
piso	**3.**	floor
sillón/silla de brazos	**4.**	armchair
mesita/esquinera/mesilla	**5.**	end table
lámpara/	**6.**	lamp
lámpara de mesa		
pantalla	**7.**	lampshade
ventana	**8.**	window
cortinas	**9.**	drapes/curtains
sofá	**10.**	sofa/couch
cojín	**11.**	pillow
cielo raso	**12.**	ceiling
pared	**13.**	wall
mueble/mueble de pared/	**14.**	wall unit/
unidad de módulos/		entertainment unit
centro de entretenimiento		
televisor	**15.**	television
videograbadora/	**16.**	video cassette
videoreproductora		recorder/VCR
estéreo/	**17.**	stereo system
equipo estereofónico		
bocina	**18.**	speaker
canapé/sofá pequeño	**19.**	loveseat
mata/planta	**20.**	plant
cuadro	**21.**	painting
marco	**22.**	frame
repisa	**23.**	mantel
hogar/chimenea	**24.**	fireplace
rejilla (para la chimenea)	**25.**	fireplace screen
foto/fotografía/retrato	**26.**	picture/photograph
librera/librero/	**27.**	bookcase
estante para libros		

A. Where are you?
B. I'm in the living room.
A. What are you doing?
B. I'm *dusting** the **coffee table**.

*dusting/cleaning

Tell about your living room.
(In my living room there's
............)

mesa de comedor **1.** (dining room) table

silla/silla de comedor **2.** (dining room) chair

vitrina/chinero/ **3.** china cabinet
alacena para la loza

vajilla/vajilla de **4.** china
porcelana/vajilla de loza

lámpara de araña/de **5.** chandelier
techo/candil de techo

aparador **6.** buffet

ensaladera **7.** salad bowl

jarra **8.** pitcher

fuente honda/sopera **9.** serving bowl

bandeja **10.** serving platter

mantel **11.** tablecloth

candelero **12.** candlestick

vela **13.** candle

centro de mesa **14.** centerpiece

salero **15.** salt shaker

pimentero **16.** pepper shaker

mantequillera **17.** butter dish

carrito de servir **18.** serving cart

tetera **19.** teapot

cafetera **20.** coffee pot

jarrita para la leche/ **21.** creamer
para la crema/lechera/
cremera

azucarera **22.** sugar bowl

A. This **dining room table** is very nice.
B. Thank you. It was a gift from my *grandmother.**

*grandmother/grandfather/
aunt/uncle/...

Tell about your dining room. (In my dining room there's ....)

plato para la ensalada	**1.** salad plate
platito para el pan y la mantequilla	**2.** bread-and-butter plate
plato	**3.** dinner plate
plato para la sopa/plato hondo	**4.** soup bowl
vaso	**5.** water glass
copa	**6.** wine glass
taza	**7.** cup
platito/platillo	**8.** saucer
servilleta	**9.** napkin

vajilla de plata/vajilla de cubiertos/juego de cubiertos	**silverware**
tenedor para la ensalada/ para el primer plato	**10.** salad fork
tenedor/trinche	**11.** dinner fork
cuchillo	**12.** knife
cucharita/cucharilla	**13.** teaspoon
cuchara	**14.** soup spoon
cuchillo para la mantequilla	**15.** butter knife

A. Excuse me. Where does the **salad plate** go?
B. It goes *to the left of* the **dinner plate**.

A. Excuse me. Where does the **soup spoon** go?
B. It goes *to the right of* the **teaspoon**.

A. Excuse me. Where does the **wine glass** go?
B. It goes *between* the **water glass** and the **cup and saucer**.

A. Excuse me. Where does the **cup** go?
B. It goes *on* the **saucer**.

Practice giving directions. Tell someone how to set a table. (Put the ....)

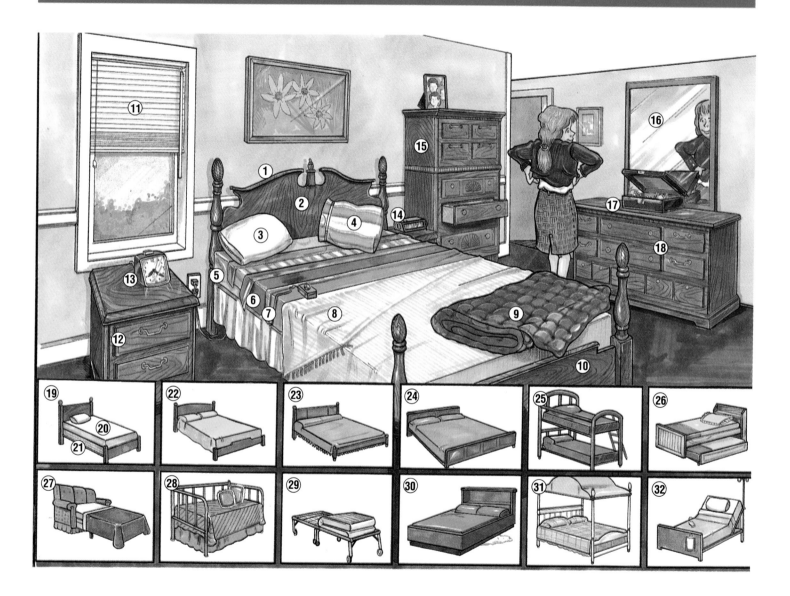

Spanish	#	English
cama	1.	bed
cabecera	2.	headboard
almohada	3.	pillow
funda	4.	pillowcase
sábana	5.	sheet
manta/cobija/frisa	6.	blanket
manta/frisa eléctrica	7.	electric blanket
sobrecama/cubrecama/colcha/frazada	8.	bedspread
edredón	9.	comforter/quilt
pie de la cama	10.	footboard
persianas	11.	blinds
mesita de noche	12.	night table/nightstand
despertador	13.	alarm clock
radio reloj/despertador	14.	clock radio
ropero/gavetero/gavatera/chifonier	15.	chest (of drawers)
espejo	16.	mirror
joyero	17.	jewelry box
cómoda/tocador/chiforobe	18.	dresser/bureau
cama gemela/sencilla/individual	19.	twin bed
colchón	20.	mattress
colchón de muelles	21.	box spring
cama doble/camera	22.	double bed
cama de matrimonio/doble/doble cama	23.	queen-size bed
cama tamaño king/cama gigante	24.	king-size bed
cama litera/cama camarote	25.	bunk bed
cama nido	26.	trundle bed
sofá cama	27.	sofa bed/convertible sofa
canapé	28.	day bed
catre	29.	cot
cama con colchón de agua	30.	water bed
cama con baldaquín(o)/con tolda	31.	canopy bed
cama de hospital	32.	hospital bed

A. Ooh! Look at that big bug!!
B. Where?
A. It's on the **bed**!
B. I'LL get it.

Tell about your bedroom. (In my bedroom there's ....)

lavaplatos/lavadora de platos	**1.**	dishwasher
jabón para la lavadora de platos	**2.**	dishwasher detergent
jabón liquido para lavar platos	**3.**	dishwashing liquid
llave/grifo/pluma	**4.**	faucet
fregador/fregadero	**5.**	sink
triturador de desperdicios	**6.**	(garbage) disposal
esponja	**7.**	sponge
estropajo/brillo	**8.**	scouring pad
cepillo para restregar ollas	**9.**	pot scrubber
escurreplatos	**10.**	dish rack
colgador para papel de toalla	**11.**	paper towel holder
trapo/paño/toalla de cocina	**12.**	dish towel
compresor de basura	**13.**	trash compactor
gabinete	**14.**	cabinet
horno microondas	**15.**	microwave
mostrador	**16.**	counter
tablita/tabla para picar/picador	**17.**	cutting board

lata/envase para harina, azúcar, té o sal	**18.**	canister
estufa/cocina/hornillo	**19.**	stove/range
horno	**20.**	oven
agarrador de ollas	**21.**	potholder
tostadora	**22.**	toaster
tablilla para especias/especiero	**23.**	spice rack
abridor de latas (eléctrico)	**24.**	can opener
libro de recetas de cocina	**25.**	cookbook
refrigerador/refrigeradora	**26.**	refrigerator
congelador	**27.**	freezer
dispensador de hielo automático	**28.**	ice maker
bandeja/cubeta de hielo	**29.**	ice tray
mesa	**30.**	kitchen table
mantelito individual	**31.**	placemat
silla	**32.**	kitchen chair
cubo/bote de basura/ basurero/ tinaco/zafacón	**33.**	garbage pail

A. I think we need a new **dishwasher**.
B. I think you're right.

Tell about your kitchen.
(In my kitchen there's
............)

Spanish		English	
peluche/osito de peluche	**1.** teddy bear	sonajero/sonajera/ sonaja/maraquita	**14.** rattle
intercomunicador	**2.** intercom	cuna/cuna mecedora	**15.** cradle
gavetero/gavetera/ropero	**3.** chest (of drawers)	andadera/pollera/anador	**16.** walker
cuna	**4.** crib	asiento/portabebé/moisés	**17.** car seat
móvil	**5.** mobile	carrito/carriola/coche	**18.** stroller
lamparita/lamparilla/lucecita	**6.** night light	coche/cochecito/carricoche	**19.** baby carriage
camilla/mesa para cambiar pañales	**7.** changing table/ dressing table	plato térmico/termo para bebés	**20.** food warmer
cubo/bote/zafacón para pañales	**8.** diaper pail	sillita elevadora	**21.** booster seat
baúl para juguetes	**9.** toy chest	sillita de infante/ portabebé/moisés	**22.** baby seat
muñeca	**10.** doll	trona/silla alta para bebés	**23.** high chair
columpio	**11.** swing	cuna portátil	**24.** portable crib
corral	**12.** playpen	portabebé	**25.** baby carrier
peluche/muñeco/ muñeca de trapo	**13.** stuffed animal	bacinilla/bacenilla/bacín	**26.** potty

A. Thank you for the **teddy bear**.
 It's a very nice gift.
B. You're welcome.

Tell about your country:
What things do people buy for a new baby? Does a new baby sleep in a separate room, as in the United States?

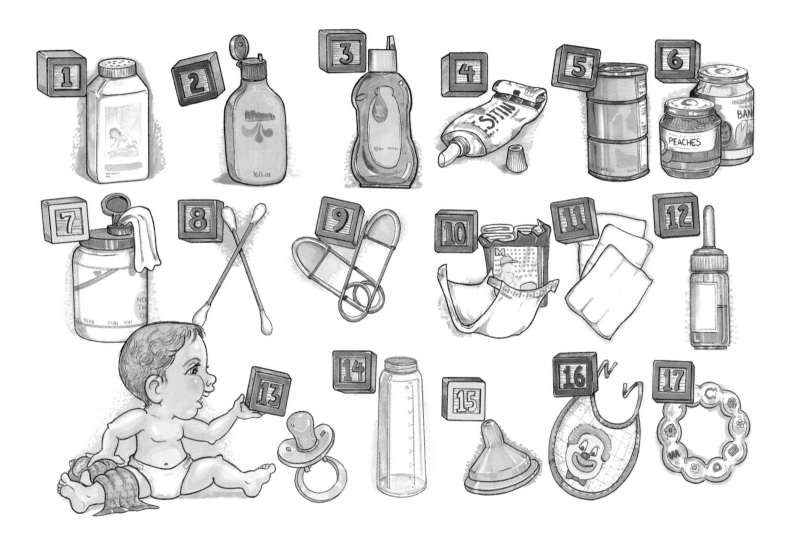

polvo/talco para niños **1.** baby powder

loción para niños **2.** baby lotion

champú para niños **3.** baby shampoo

ungüento **4.** ointment

fórmula **5.** formula

papillas/alimentos para niños/colados **6.** baby food

servilletas/toallitas desechables **7.** (baby) wipes

palitos/palillos de algodón/hisopos/hisopillos **8.** cotton swabs

alfileres/imperdibles **9.** diaper pins

pañales desechables **10.** disposable diapers

pañales de tela/de algodón **11.** cloth diapers

vitaminas en líquido/en gotas **12.** (liquid) vitamins

chupón/chupete/chupador/consuelo/bobo **13.** pacifier

mamadera/biberón/tetero **14.** bottle

mamadera/tetina/tetilla **15.** nipple

babero **16.** bib

chupador **17.** teething ring

[1–12]
A. Do we need anything from the store?
B. Yes. Please get some more **baby powder**.

[13–17]
A. Do we need anything from the store?
B. Yes. Please get another **pacifier**.

Tell about baby products in your country.

bomba destapacaños/ desatascador — **1.** plunger

inodoro/taza de escusado/ tazón/retrete — **2.** toilet

redondela/silla del inodoro — **3.** toilet seat

desodorante/desodorizador/ aromatizante ambiental — **4.** air freshener

papel higiénico — **5.** toilet paper

cepillo — **6.** toilet brush

toallero — **7.** towel rack

toalla — **8.** towel

canasta/cesto para la ropa sucia — **9.** hamper

pesa — **10.** scale

secadora de cabello/de pelo — **11.** hair dryer

ventilador/abanico eléctrico — **12.** fan

espejo — **13.** mirror

botiquín/gabinete — **14.** medicine cabinet/ medicine chest

lavabo/lavamanos — **15.** sink

llave/pluma de agua — **16.** faucet

cepillo de dientes — **17.** toothbrush

jabón — **18.** soap

dispensador de jabón — **19.** soap dispenser

sistema de higiene dental a presión de agua — **20.** Water Pik

gabinete/mueble — **21.** vanity

cesto/canasta para la basura — **22.** wastebasket

regadera/ducha/baño — **23.** shower

cortina de baño — **24.** shower curtain

tina/bañera — **25.** bathtub/tub

desagüe — **26.** drain

parche antirresbalón/ alfombrilla/estera de goma — **27.** rubber mat

esponja — **28.** sponge

alfombra de baño — **29.** bath mat

A. Where's the **plunger**?
B. It's *next to* the **toilet**.

A. Where's the **mirror**?
B. It's *over* the **sink**.

A. Where's the **towel**?
B. It's *on* the **towel rack**.

Tell about your bathroom.
(In my bathroom there's
............)

cepillo de dientes	1.	toothbrush
peine/peinilla	2.	comb
cepillo para el cabello/el pelo	3.	brush
máquina de afeitar/de rasurar	4.	razor
navaja	5.	razor blades
máquina de afeitar/de rasurar eléctrica	6.	electric razor/electric shaver
gorra(o) de baño	7.	shower cap
cortauñas	8.	nail clipper
tijeras	9.	scissors
pinzas de sacar cejas	10.	tweezers
champú	11.	shampoo
enjuage/acondicionador	12.	conditioner
fijador para el cabello	13.	hairspray
talco/polvo	14.	powder
pasta de dientes/crema dental	15.	toothpaste
antiséptico/enjuague bucal	16.	mouthwash
seda/hilo dental	17.	dental floss
crema para afeitarse/para rasurarse/de afeitar	18.	shaving creme
crema refrescante	19.	after shave lotion
deodorante/desodorante	20.	deodorant
perfume/colonia	21.	perfume/cologne
esmalte de uñas	22.	nail polish
lápiz de labio/carmín	23.	lipstick
betún/pasta lustradora para zapatos	24.	shoe polish
maquillaje	25.	makeup

[1–10]
A. Excuse me. Where can I find **toothbrush**es?
B. They're in the next aisle.
A. Thank you.

[11–25]
A. Excuse me. Where can I find **shampoo**?
B. It's in the next aisle.
A. Thank you.

You're going on a trip. Make a list of personal care products you need to take with you.

escoba	**1.** broom		tina para lavar	**11.** utility sink
recogedor	**2.** dustpan		esponja	**12.** sponge
plancha	**3.** iron		basurero/bote para basura/ tinaco/zafacón	**13.** trash can/ garbage can
tabla de (a)planchar	**4.** ironing board			
aspiradora	**5.** vacuum cleaner		canasta para la ropa sucia	**14.** laundry basket
aspiradora de mano/ aspiradora portátil	**6.** hand vacuum		cubo/cubeta	**15.** bucket/pail
			cepillo para limpiar el inodoro	**16.** scrub brush
trapeador	**7.** mop		caja para artículos renovables/reciclables	**17.** recycling bin
lavadora	**8.** washing machine/ washer			
			cordón/cuerda/soga para tender ropa	**18.** clothesline
secadora	**9.** dryer			
papel toalla/papel absorbente	**10.** paper towels		horquillas/pinzas/pinches/ ganchos para tender ropa	**19.** clothespins

A. Excuse me. Do you sell **brooms**?
B. Yes. They're at the back of the store.
A. Thanks.

Who does the cleaning and laundry in your home? What things does that person use?

farol	**1.** lamppost
casilla/casillero postal	**2.** mailbox
porche/portal	**3.** front porch
puerta principal	**4.** front door
timbre	**5.** doorbell
ventana	**6.** window
contraventana/postigo	**7.** shutter
tejado/techo	**8.** roof
antena de televisión	**9.** TV antenna
chimenea	**10.** chimney
garaje/estacionamiento/cochera	**11.** garage

puerta del garaje/puerta del estacionamiento/puerta de la cochera	**12.** garage door
entrada para el coche/para el carro	**13.** driveway
plataforma/terraza/asoleadera	**14.** deck
puerta de atrás	**15.** back door
antena parabólica	**16.** satellite dish
patio	**17.** patio
cortacésped/cortagrama/máquina cortadora de césped/de grama/de zacate	**18.** lawnmower
barbacoa/parrilla	**19.** barbecue/grill
barraca/caseta para herramientas	**20.** tool shed

A. When are you going to repair the **lamppost**?
B. I'm going to repair it tomorrow.

Do you like to repair things?
What things can you repair yourself?
What things can't you repair?
Who repairs them?

vestíbulo	**1.**	lobby
portero automático/eléctrico	**2.**	intercom
timbre/zumbador/chicharra	**3.**	buzzer
casillero postal	**4.**	mailbox
ascensor/elevador	**5.**	elevator
detector de humo	**6.**	smoke detector
mirilla	**7.**	peephole
cadena antirrobo/ de seguridad	**8.**	door chain
cerradura/pestillo	**9.**	lock
aire acondicionado	**10.**	air conditioner
alarma contra incendios	**11.**	fire alarm
disparador/ducto de basura/ conducto para la basura	**12.**	garbage chute
lavandería	**13.**	laundry room
conserje/supervisor/super	**14.**	superintendent
depósito	**15.**	storage room
garaje/estacionamiento con techo	**16.**	parking garage
estacionamiento	**17.**	parking lot
balcón/terraza	**18.**	balcony
piscina/alberca/pileta	**19.**	swimming pool
bañera de hidromasaje/de terapia/tina de terapia/ tina-jacuzzi	**20.**	whirlpool

A. Is there a **lobby**?
B. Yes, there is. Do you want to see the apartment?
A. Yes, please.

Tell about the differences between living in a house and in an apartment building.

carpintero	**1.** carpenter	la cuenta del gas	**12.** gas bill
ayudante	**2.** handyman	la cuenta de la electricidad	**13.** electric bill
pintor	**3.** painter	la cuenta del teléfono	**14.** telephone bill
deshollinador	**4.** chimney sweep	la cuenta del agua	**15.** water bill
reparador de electrodomésticos	**5.** appliance repair person	la cuenta de la calefacción	**16.** oil bill/heating bill
reparador de televisión	**6.** TV repair person	la cuenta del cable	**17.** cable TV bill
cerrajero	**7.** locksmith	la cuenta de la fumigación	**18.** pest control bill
jardinero	**8.** gardener	alquiler	**19.** rent
electricista	**9.** electrician	mensualidad/cuota para el estacionamiento	**20.** parking fee
plomero	**10.** plumber	hipoteca	**21.** mortgage payment
fumigador	**11.** exterminator		

A. Did you pay the **carpenter**?
B. Yes. I wrote a check yesterday.

Tell about utilities, services, and repairs you pay for. How much do you pay?

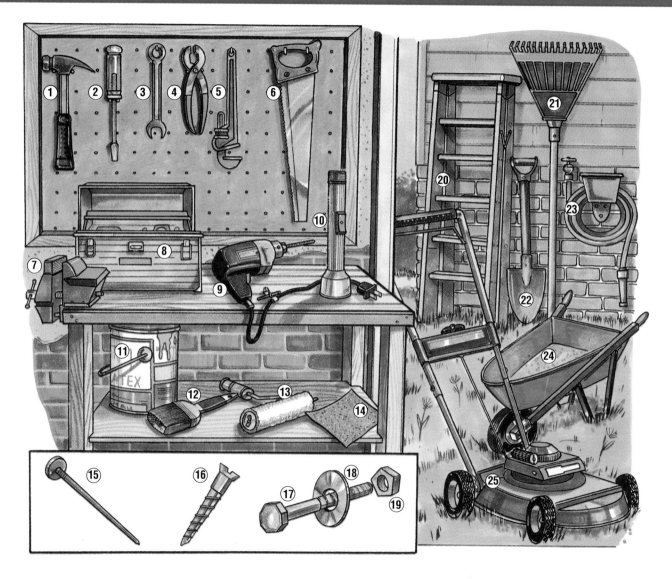

martillo	**1.** hammer	lija	**14.** sandpaper
destornillador	**2.** screwdriver	clavo	**15.** nail
llave inglesa/para tuercas	**3.** wrench	tornillo	**16.** screw
alicates/pinzas	**4.** pliers	perno	**17.** bolt
llave inglesa	**5.** monkey wrench	arandela	**18.** washer
serrucho	**6.** saw	tuerca	**19.** nut
torno/tornillo/prensa de banco	**7.** vise	escalera	**20.** step ladder
caja de herramientas	**8.** toolbox	rastrillo	**21.** rake
barrena/taladro eléctrico	**9.** electric drill	pala	**22.** shovel
linterna/lámpara/faro de mano	**10.** flashlight	manguera	**23.** hose
pintura	**11.** paint	carretilla	**24.** wheelbarrow
brocha	**12.** paintbrush	cortacésped/cortagrama/ máquina cortadora	**25.** lawnmower
rodillo	**13.** paint roller		

A. Can I borrow your **hammer***?
B. Sure.
A. Thanks.

*With 11 and 14, use: Can I borrow
   some _____?
*With 15–19, use: Can I borrow
   some _____s?

Do you like to work
   with tools?
What tools do you
   have in your home?

1 one	11 eleven	21 twenty-one	101 one hundred (and) one
2 two	12 twelve	22 twenty-two	102 one hundred (and) two
3 three	13 thirteen	30 thirty	1,000 one thousand
4 four	14 fourteen	40 forty	10,000 ten thousand
5 five	15 fifteen	50 fifty	100,000 one hundred thousand
6 six	16 sixteen	60 sixty	1,000,000 one million
7 seven	17 seventeen	70 seventy	
8 eight	18 eighteen	80 eighty	
9 nine	19 nineteen	90 ninety	
10 ten	20 twenty	100 one hundred	

A. How old are you?
B. I'm _____ years old.

A. How many people are there in your family?
B. _____.

1st	first	11th	eleventh	21st	twenty-first	101st	one hundred (and) first
2nd	second	12th	twelfth	22nd	twenty-second	102nd	one hundred (and) second
3rd	third	13th	thirteenth	30th	thirtieth	1000th	one thousandth
4th	fourth	14th	fourteenth	40th	fortieth	10,000th	ten thousandth
5th	fifth	15th	fifteenth	50th	fiftieth	100,000th	one hundred thousandth
6th	sixth	16th	sixteenth	60th	sixtieth	1,000,000th	one millionth
7th	seventh	17th	seventeenth	70th	seventieth		
8th	eighth	18th	eighteenth	80th	eightieth		
9th	ninth	19th	nineteenth	90th	ninetieth		
10th	tenth	20th	twentieth	100th	one hundredth		

A. What floor do you live on?
B. I live on the _____ floor.

A. Is this the first time you've seen this movie?
B. No. It's the _____ time.

Aritmética/**Arithmetic**

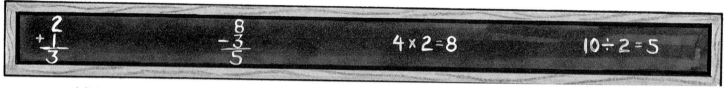

suma addition
2 **plus** 1 **equals*** 3.
You can also say:* **is

resta subtraction
8 **minus** 3 **equals*** 5.

multiplicacíon multiplication
4 **times** 2 **equals*** 8.

divisíon division
10 **divided by** 2 **equals*** 5.

Fracciones/**Fractions**

 ¼

one quarter/
one fourth

 ⅓

one third

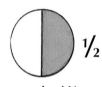 ½

one half/
half

 ⅔

two thirds

 ¾

three quarters/
three fourths

Por cientos/**Percents**

 25%

twenty-five percent

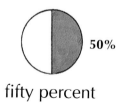 50%

fifty percent

 75%

seventy-five percent

 100%

one hundred percent

A. How much is two plus one?
B. Two plus one equals/is three.

Make conversations for the arithmetic problems at the top of page 50. Then make other conversations.

A. Is this on sale?
B. Yes. It's _____ off the regular price.

A. Is the gas tank almost empty?
B. It's about _____ full.

A. How did you do on the test?
B. I got _____ percent of the answers right.

A. What's the weather forecast?
B. There's a _____ percent chance of rain.

 **2:00**

two o'clock

 2:15

two fifteen
a quarter after *two*

 **2:30**

two thirty
half past *two*

 **2:45**

two forty-five
a quarter to *three*

 **2:05**

two oh five

 **2:20**

two twenty
twenty after *two*

 **2:40**

two forty
twenty to *three*

 **2:55**

two fifty-five
five to *three*

A. What time is it?
B. It's _____.

A. What time does the movie begin?
B. At _____.

| two a.m. | two p.m. | noon
twelve noon | midnight
twelve midnight |

A. When does the train leave?
B. At _____.

A. What time will we arrive?
B. At _____.

Tell about your daily schedule:
   What do you do?
   When?
   (I get up at _____.
   I ....)

Tell about time in different cultures or countries you are familiar with:
   Do people arrive on time for work? appointments? parties?
   Do trains and buses run on schedule?
   Do movies and sports events begin on time?
   Do workplaces use time clocks or timesheets?

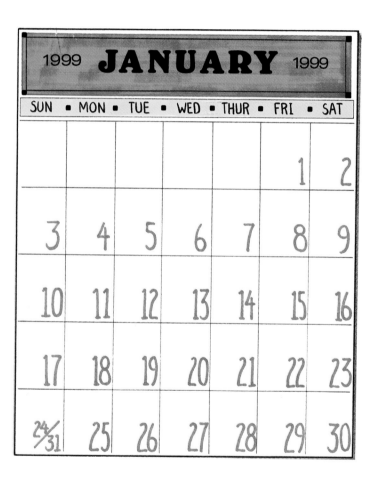

año	**1.**	**year**
mil novecientos noventa y nueve		nineteen ninety-nine
mes	**2.**	**month**
enero		January
febrero		February
marzo		March
abril		April
mayo		May
junio		June
julio		July
agosto		August
septiembre		September
octubre		October
noviembre		November
diciembre		December
día	**3.**	**day**
domingo		Sunday
lunes		Monday
martes		Tuesday
miércoles		Wednesday
jueves		Thursday
viernes		Friday
sábado		Saturday
fecha	**4.**	**date**
2 de enero de 1999		January 2, 1999
2/1/99		1/2/99
dos de enero de mil novecientos noventa y nueve		January second, nineteen ninety-nine

A. What year is it?
B. It's _____.

A. What month is it?
B. It's _____.

A. What day is it?
B. It's _____.

A. What's today's date?
B. Today is _____.

When did you begin to study English?
What days of the week do you study English?
   (I study English on _____.)

When is your birthday? (My birthday is on _____.)
What is your favorite month of the year? Why?

panadería/pastelería/repostería	**1.** bakery
banco	**2.** bank
barbería	**3.** barber shop
librería	**4.** book store
estación/terminal de autobuses	**5.** bus station
cafetería	**6.** cafeteria
guardería infantil	**7.** child-care center/day-care center
tintorería/lavandería en seco	**8.** cleaners
clínica	**9.** clinic
cafetería	**10.** coffee shop
tienda/tiendita/tanquería	**11.** convenience store

A. Where are you going?
B. I'm going to the **bakery**.

Which of these places are in your neighborhood? (In my neighborhood there's a ....)

almacén	**1.** department store	salón de belleza/peluquería	**6.** hair salon
farmacia	**2.** drug store/pharmacy	ferretería	**7.** hardware store
floristería	**3.** flower shop/florist	gimnasio/club	**8.** health club
gasolinera/surtidor/ estación de gasolina	**4.** gas station/ service station	hospital	**9.** hospital
tienda/abarrotería/ bodega/colmado	**5.** grocery store	hotel	**10.** hotel

A. Hi! How are you today?
B. Fine. Where are you going?
A. To the **department store**. How about you?
B. I'm going to the **drug store**.

Which of these places are in your neighborhood? (In my neighborhood there's a ....)

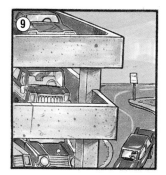

heladería/refresquería/ sorbetería **1.** ice cream shop

lavamático/lavandería pública **2.** laundromat

biblioteca **3.** library

motel **4.** motel

cine **5.** movie theater

museo **6.** museum

almacén/tienda de música **7.** music store

parque **8.** park

estacionamiento/garaje **9.** parking garage

estacionamiento **10.** parking lot

tienda de animales domésticos/ de mascotas **11.** pet shop

pizzería **12.** pizza shop

A. Where's the **ice cream shop**?
B. It's right over there.

Which of these places are in your neighborhood? (In my neighborhood there's a/an ....)

edificio/oficina de correos/el correo	**1.** post office
restaurante	**2.** restaurant
escuela	**3.** school
zapatería/tienda de zapatos	**4.** shoe store
centro comercial	**5.** shopping mall
supermercado	**6.** supermarket
teatro	**7.** theater
juguetería	**8.** toy store
estación del tren	**9.** train station
videocentro	**10.** video store
zoológico	**11.** zoo

A. Is there a **post office** nearby?

B. Yes. There's a **post office** around the corner.

Which of these places are in your neighborhood? (In my neighborhood there's a ....)

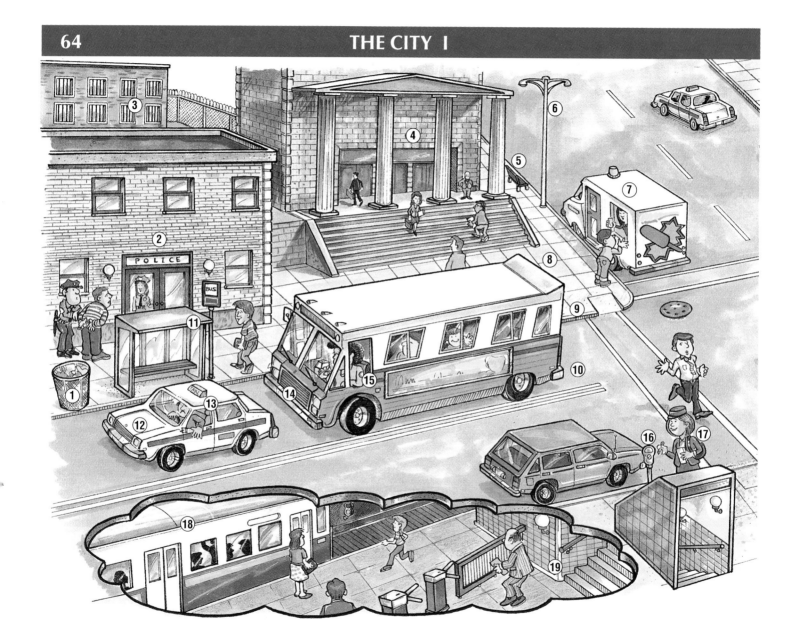

basurero **1.** trash container

estación de policía **2.** police station

cárcel **3.** jail

juzgado/corte/tribunal **4.** courthouse

banca/banco **5.** bench

farol **6.** street light

repartidor de helados/ **7.** ice cream truck
carretilla de helados

acera **8.** sidewalk

cuneta/cubeta **9.** curb

calle **10.** street

parada/paradero de **11.** bus stop
autobuses/de guaguas

taxi **12.** taxi/cab

taxista/conductor(a)/ **13.** taxi driver/
chofer de taxi cab driver

autobús/bus/guagua/camión **14.** bus

busero(a)/conductor(a)/ **15.** bus driver
chofer de autobús

parquímetro/estacionómetro **16.** parking meter

inspectora de estacionómetro **17.** meter maid

subterráneo/metro **18.** subway

estación del metro **19.** subway station

A. Where's the _____?
B. On/In/Next to/Between/
Across from/In front of/
Behind/Under/Over
the _____.

Which of these people, places, and things are in your neighborhood?

1
2
3
4
5
6
7
8
9
10
11
12
13
14
15
16
TAXI
ENGINE UNIT No 5
MAIN ST
CENTER

parada de taxis/piquera **1.** taxi stand

cabina de teléfonos **2.** phone booth

teléfono público **3.** public telephone

letrero con el nombre de la calle **4.** street sign

estación de bomberos **5.** fire station

edificio de oficinas **6.** office building

cajero rápido/ventanilla de servicio rápido **7.** drive-through window

alarma de incendios **8.** fire alarm box

cruce **9.** intersection

policía **10.** police officer

vía/paso peatonal/cruce de peatones/ línea de seguridad **11.** crosswalk

peatón **12.** pedestrian

semáforo **13.** traffic light

camión de la basura **14.** garbage truck

puesto de periódicos **15.** newsstand

buhonero/vendedor ambulante **16.** street vendor

A. Where's the _____?
B. On/In/Next to/Between/ Across from/In front of/ Behind/Under/Over the _____.

Which of these people, places, and things are in your neighborhood?

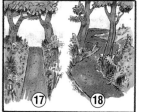

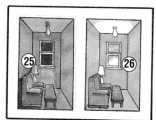

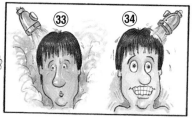

alto(a) – bajo(a)	**1–2**	tall – short	1–2	Is your sister _____?
largo(a) – corto(a)	**3–4**	long – short	3–4	Is his hair _____?
grande – chiquito(a)/pequeño(a)	**5–6**	large/big – small/little	5–6	Is their dog _____?
alto(a) – bajo(a)	**7–8**	high – low	7–8	Is the bridge _____?
gordo(a) – flaco(a)	**9–10**	heavy/fat – thin/skinny	9–10	Is your friend _____?
pesado(a) – liviano(a)	**11–12**	heavy – light	11–12	Is the box _____?
flojo(a) – estrecho(a)/apretado(a)	**13–14**	loose – tight	13–14	Are the pants _____?
rápido(a) – lento(a)	**15–16**	fast – slow	15–16	Is the train _____?
recto(a) – curvo(a)	**17–18**	straight – crooked	17–18	Is the path _____?
liso(a) – rizado(a)	**19–20**	straight – curly	19–20	Is his hair _____?
ancho(a) – angosto(a)/estrecho(a)	**21–22**	wide – narrow	21–22	Is that street _____?
grueso(a) – delgado(a)	**23–24**	thick – thin	23–24	Is the line _____?
oscuro(a) – claro(a)/con luz	**25–26**	dark – light	25–26	Is the room _____?
nuevo(a) – viejo(a)	**27–28**	new – old	27–28	Is your car _____?
joven – viejo(a)	**29–30**	young – old	29–30	Is he _____?
bueno(a)(s) – malo(a)(s)	**31–32**	good – bad	31–32	Are your neighbor's children _____?
caliente – frío(a)	**33–34**	hot – cold	33–34	Is the water _____?

[1–2]
A. Is your sister **tall**?
B. No. She's **short**.

Describe yourself.
Describe a person
  you know.
Describe one of your
  favorite places.

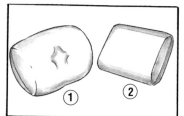

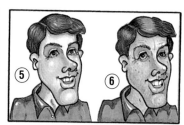

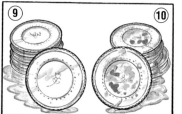

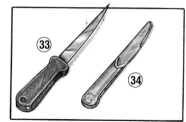

suave – duro(a)	**1–2**	soft – hard	1–2	Is your pillow _____?
fácil – difícil	**3–4**	easy – difficult/hard	3–4	Is today's homework _____?
liso(a) – áspero(a)	**5–6**	smooth – rough	5–6	Is your skin _____?
ordenado(a) – desordenado(a)	**7–8**	neat – messy	7–8	Is your desk _____?
limpio(a) – sucio(a)	**9–10**	clean – dirty	9–10	Are the dishes _____?
escandaloso(a) – quieto(a)/	**11–12**	noisy/loud – quiet	11–12	Is your neighbor _____?
tranquilo(a)/callado(a)			13–14	Is your sister _____?
casado(a) – soltero(a)	**13–14**	married – single	15–16	Is your uncle _____?
rico/adinerado – pobre	**15–16**	rich/wealthy – poor	17–18	Is the witch _____?
bonito(a) – feo(a)	**17–18**	pretty/beautiful – ugly	19–20	Is the pirate _____?
guapo(a) – feo(a)	**19–20**	handsome – ugly	21–22	Are the clothes _____?
mojado(a) – seco(a)	**21–22**	wet – dry	23–24	Is the door _____?
abierto(a) – cerrado(a)	**23–24**	open – closed	25–26	Is the pitcher _____?
lleno(a) – vacío(a)	**25–26**	full – empty	27–28	Is that restaurant _____?
caro(a) – barato(a)	**27–28**	expensive – cheap/inexpensive	29–30	Is the dress _____?
elegante/adornado(a)–sencillo(a)	**29–30**	fancy – plain	31–32	Is your kitchen floor _____?
brillante – opaco(a)	**31–32**	shiny – dull	33–34	Is the knife _____?
afilado(a) – romo(a)	**33–34**	sharp – dull		

[1–2]
A. Is your pillow **soft**?
B. No. It's **hard**.

Describe yourself.
Describe a person
  you know.
Describe one of your
  favorite places.

cansado(a)	**1.** tired	enfermo(a)	**7.** sick
tener calor	**2.** hot	contento(a)	**8.** happy
tener frío	**3.** cold	triste	**9.** sad/unhappy
tener hambre	**4.** hungry	decepcionado(a)	**10.** disappointed
tener sed/sediento	**5.** thirsty	contrariado(a)	**11.** upset
estar lleno	**6.** full	molesto(a)/contrariado(a)	**12.** annoyed

A. You look **tired**.
B. I am. I'm VERY **tired**.

What makes you happy?
What makes you sad?
When do you get annoyed?

frustrado(a)	**1.** frustrated		asustado(a)/con miedo	**7.** scared/afraid
furioso(a)/enfadado(a)/disgustado(a)	**2.** angry/mad		aburrido(a)	**8.** bored
harto(a)/colmado(a)/asqueado	**3.** disgusted		orgulloso(a)	**9.** proud
sorprendido(a)	**4.** surprised		avergonzado(a)	**10.** embarrassed
nervioso(a)	**5.** nervous		celoso(a)	**11.** jealous
preocupado(a)	**6.** worried		enredado(a)/confundido(a)	**12.** confused

A. Are you **frustrated**?
B. Yes. I'm VERY **frustrated**.

What makes you angry? What makes you nervous? Do you ever feel embarrassed? When?

manzana	**1.** apple		sandía/melón de agua	**17.** watermelon
melocotón	**2.** peach		toronja	**18.** grapefruit
pera	**3.** pear		limón (amarillo)	**19.** lemon
banana/guineo/plátano	**4.** banana		lima/limón verde	**20.** lime
ciruela	**5.** plum		naranja/china	**21.** orange
albaricoque	**6.** apricot		mandarina	**22.** tangerine
nectarina	**7.** nectarine		uvas	**23.** grapes
kiwi	**8.** kiwi		cerezas	**24.** cherries
papaya/fruta bomba	**9.** papaya		ciruelas pasas	**25.** prunes
mango	**10.** mango		dátiles	**26.** dates
higo	**11.** fig		uvas pasas/pasitas	**27.** raisins
coco	**12.** coconut		arándano	**28.** blueberries
aguacate	**13.** avocado		arándano agrio	**29.** cranberries
melón	**14.** cantaloupe		frambuesas	**30.** raspberries
melón verde/dulce	**15.** honeydew		fresas	**31.** strawberries
piña	**16.** pineapple			

[1–22]

A. This **apple** is delicious!
B. I'm glad you like it.

[23–31]

A. These **grapes** are delicious!
B. I'm glad you like them.

What fruits do you like?
Which of these fruits grow
   where you live?
What other fruits do you
   know?

lechuga	**1.**	lettuce
repollo/col	**2.**	cabbage
apio	**3.**	celery
maíz/elote	**4.**	corn
coliflor	**5.**	cauliflower
brócoli/brécol	**6.**	broccoli
espinaca	**7.**	spinach
espárrago	**8.**	asparagus
berenjena	**9.**	eggplant
calabacita/calabacín	**10.**	zucchini
calabaza pequeña	**11.**	acorn squash
zapallo	**12.**	butternut squash
guisante/chícharo/petit pois	**13.**	pea
habichuelas tiernas/ ejotes/judías verdes	**14.**	string bean/ green bean
haba	**15.**	lima bean
frijol negro	**16.**	black bean
frijol rojo/habichuelas coloradas	**17.**	kidney bean
repollito/col de bruselas	**18.**	brussels sprout

pepino/pepinillo	**19.**	cucumber
tomate	**20.**	tomato
zanahoria	**21.**	carrot
rábano	**22.**	radish
hongo/seta	**23.**	mushroom
alcachofa	**24.**	artichoke
papa/patata	**25.**	potato
boniato/camote/batata	**26.**	sweet potato
papa dulce/batata	**27.**	yam
pimiento verde	**28.**	green pepper
pimiento rojo/ pimiento morron	**29.**	red pepper
remolacha	**30.**	beet
cebolla	**31.**	onion
cebollino(a)/cebollin/ escalonia	**32.**	scallion/green onion
cebolla morada	**33.**	red onion
cebollita/cebolla blanca	**34.**	pearl onion
nabo	**35.**	turnip
nabo/pastinaca	**36.**	parsnip

A. What do we need from the supermarket?
B. We need **lettuce*** and **pea**s.†

*1–12   †13–36

Which vegetables do you like?
Which of these vegetables grow where you live?
What other vegetables do you know?

leche **1.** milk

leche con chocolate **2.** chocolate milk

crema **3.** cream

jugo de naranja/ **4.** orange juice
de china

queso **5.** cheese

mantequilla **6.** butter

margarina **7.** margarine

crema agria **8.** sour cream

queso crema **9.** cream cheese

requesón **10.** cottage cheese

yogur/leche búlgara **11.** yogurt

huevos **12.** eggs

A. What do we need from the supermarket?
B. We need **milk**.

Which of these foods do you like? Which foods are good for you?

mayonesa	**1.** mayonnaise		papel toalla	**17.** paper towels
salsa de tomate	**2.** ketchup		cereal	**18.** cereal
mostaza	**3.** mustard		sopa	**19.** soup
sal	**4.** salt		galletas	**20.** cookies
pimienta	**5.** pepper		jugo	**21.** juice
condimentos/especies	**6.** spices		soda/gaseosa	**22.** soda
aceite para cocinar	**7.** oil		galletas de soda	**23.** crackers
salsa china/de soya	**8.** soy sauce		torta/bizcocho	**24.** cake
vinagre	**9.** vinegar		pasta/espaguetis	**25.** spaghetti
harina	**10.** flour		arroz	**26.** rice
aliño/aderezo para ensaladas	**11.** salad dressing		fideos/tallarines	**27.** noodles
azúcar	**12.** sugar		café	**28.** coffee
pañuelos de papel/Kleenex	**13.** tissues		té	**29.** tea
servilletas	**14.** napkins		pan	**30.** bread
papel higiénico	**15.** toilet paper		panecillos	**31.** rolls
jabón	**16.** soap		helado	**32.** ice cream

A. Do we need any **mayonnaise**?
B. Yes. Let's get some.

Which of these groceries do you buy?
What brands of these products do you buy?

carne molida	**1.** ground beef	pavo	**8.** turkey
filete/biftec/bistec	**2.** steak	pescado	**9.** fish
cordero	**3.** lamb	camarones/langostinos	**10.** shrimp
puerco/cerdo	**4.** pork	almejas	**11.** clams
jamón	**5.** ham	cangrejos	**12.** crabs
tocina/tocineta	**6.** bacon	langosta	**13.** lobster
pollo	**7.** chicken		

A. Do you want to get **ground beef**?
B. Sure. Good idea.

Which of these foods do you like? What foods are good for you?

corredor/sección **1.** aisle
carretilla/carrito **2.** shopping cart
cliente **3.** shopper/customer
caja/mostrador de **4.** checkout counter
chequeo/de caja
pesa/balanza **5.** scale
caja/registradora **6.** cash register

cajero(a) **7.** cashier
bolsa plástica **8.** plastic bag
bolsa/cartucho **9.** paper bag
de papel/talego
empacador **10.** bagger/packer
fila rápida/expreso **11.** express checkout line
canasto(a)/cesto(a)/ **12.** shopping basket
bolsa/talego/cartucho

A. This is a really big supermarket!
B. It is! Look at all the **aisle**s.

Describe the differences
between U.S. supermarkets and
food stores in your country.

bolsa	**1.** bag	lata	**6.** can
barra	**2.** bar	cartón	**7.** carton
botella	**3.** bottle	envase	**8.** container
caja/cajeta/cajetita	**4.** box	docena	**9.** dozen
racimo/manojo/mazo	**5.** bunch		

A. Please get a **bag** of *flour* at the supermarket.
B. A **bag** of *flour*? Okay.

What do you do with empty bottles and cans? Do you recycle them, reuse them, or throw them away?

frasco/tarro/pote	**1.** jar		cuarto	**6.** quart
hogaza de pan	**2.** loaf-loaves		medio galón	**7.** half-gallon
paquete/bulto	**3.** package		galón	**8.** gallon
rollo	**4.** roll		litro	**9.** liter
pinta	**5.** pint		libra	**10.** pound

A. Would you get a **jar** of *mayonnaise* at the supermarket?

B. A **jar** of *mayonnaise*? Sure.

Open your kitchen cabinets and refrigerator. Make a list of all the things you find.

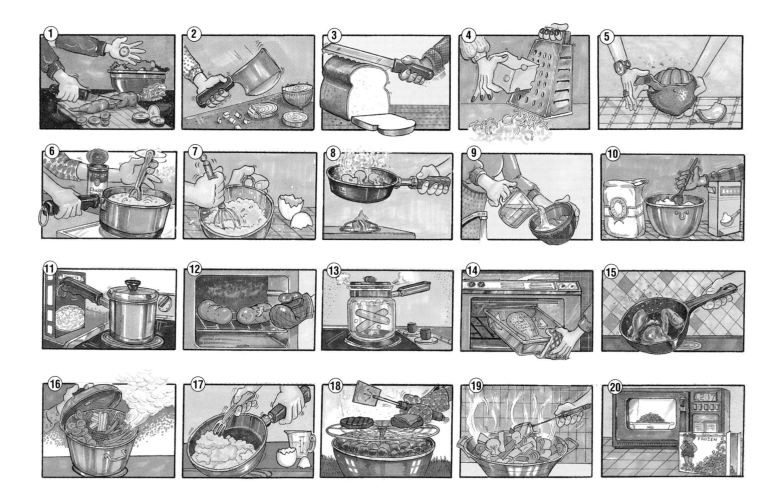

corte(a)	**1.** cut (up)
pique (pica)	**2.** chop (up)
corte(a)/rebane(a)	**3.** slice
ralle(a)	**4.** grate
pele(a)/monde(a)	**5.** peel
revuelva(e)	**6.** stir
bata(e)	**7.** beat
guise(a)/saltée (saltea)	**8.** saute
eche(a)/vierta(e)	**9.** pour
mezcle(a)	**10.** mix
cocine(a)	**11.** cook

hornée(a)	**12.** bake
hierva(e)	**13.** boil
ase(a) a la parrilla	**14.** broil
fría(e)	**15.** fry
cocine(a) al vapor/cueza (cuece) al vapor	**16.** steam
revuelva(e)	**17.** scramble
ase(a) a la parrilla	**18.** barbecue/grill
saltée (saltea)/sofría(e)	**19.** stir-fry
cueza en el microondas/ cocine(a) en el microondas	**20.** microwave

A. Can I help?
B. Yes. Please **cut up** the vegetables.

What's your favorite recipe?
Give the instructions.

buñuelo/donut/dona/llanta	**1.** donut		pizza	**10.** pizza
panecillo dulce	**2.** muffin		emparedado/sandwich	**11.** sandwich
bagel	**3.** bagel		soda/gaseosa	**12.** soda
variedad de dulces/pasteles	**4.** pastry		limonada	**13.** lemonade
bisquet/panecillo	**5.** biscuit		café	**14.** coffee
hamburguesa	**6.** hamburger		café descafeinado	**15.** decaf coffee
quesoburguesa/ hamburguesa con queso	**7.** cheeseburger		té	**16.** tea
perro caliente/hot dog	**8.** hot dog		té frío/té helado	**17.** iced tea
taco	**9.** taco		leche	**18.** milk

[1–11]

A. May I help you?

B. Yes. I'd like a **donut**, please.

[12–18]

A. What would you like to drink?

B. **Soda**.

Do you go to fast food restaurants? Which ones? What do you order?

butaca	**1.** booth	lavaplatos/lavavajillas	**7.** dishwasher
mesa	**2.** table	mozo/camarero	**8.** waiter
carta/menú	**3.** menu	moza/camarera	**9.** waitress
trona/silla alta para bebé	**4.** high chair	mozo	**10.** busboy
sillita elevadora	**5.** booster seat	cajero(a)	**11.** cashier
chef/cocinero(a)	**6.** cook		

[1–5]

A. Would you like a **booth**?

B. Yes, please.

[6–11]

A. Do you have any job openings?

B. Yes. We're looking for a **cook**.

Do you go to restaurants? Tell about a restaurant you know.

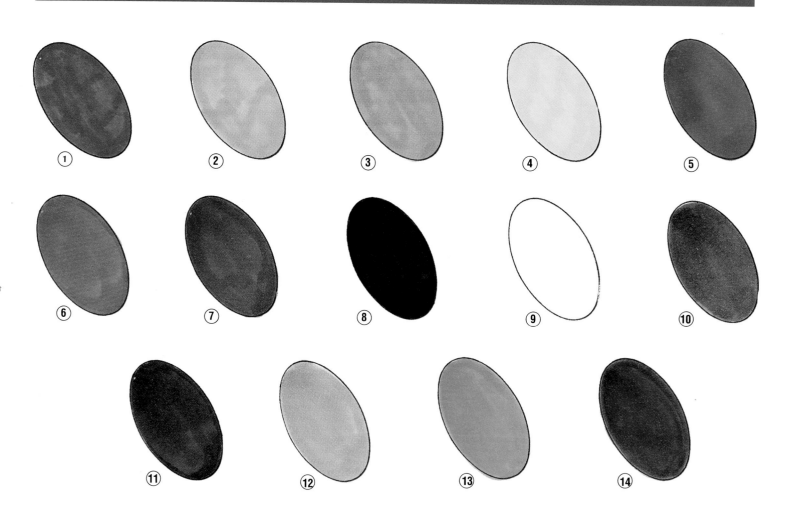

rojo	**1.** red		blanco	**9.** white
rosado/rosa	**2.** pink		gris	**10.** gray
anaranjado	**3.** orange		marrón/chocolate/pardo/ café/carmelita	**11.** brown
amarillo	**4.** yellow		crema/beige	**12.** beige
verde	**5.** green		verde claro	**13.** light green
azul	**6.** blue		verde oscuro	**14.** dark green
morado/violeta	**7.** purple			
negro	**8.** black			

A. What's your favorite color?
B. **Red.**

What are the colors of flags you know?
What color makes you happy? What color makes you sad? Why?

camisa/camisa de mangas largas	**1.** shirt		jersey/suéter cerrado/ de cuello redondo	**8.** sweater
blusa	**2.** blouse		uniforme	**9.** uniform
pantalones	**3.** pants/slacks		saco/chaqueta/chaquetón	**10.** sports jacket
pantalones de mezclila/ pantalones de dril/jeans/ mahones	**4.** jeans		traje/vestido	**11.** suit
falda	**5.** skirt		chaleco	**12.** vest
traje/vestido	**6.** dress		corbata	**13.** tie
pantalones cortos	**7.** shorts			

A. I think I'll wear my new **shirt** today.
B. Good idea!

What color clothes do you like to wear?
Do you ever wear jeans? When?

pijama	**1.** pajamas
camisón	**2.** nightgown
bata de baño/albornoz	**3.** bathrobe
zapatillas/babuchas/ chinelas/pantuflas	**4.** slippers
camiseta	**5.** undershirt
calzoncillos/ pantaloncillos/trusa	**6.** underpants
calzoncillos/pantaloncillos boxer/largos	**7.** boxer shorts
panti bikini	**8.** panties
pantis/pantaletas/ calzonarios/bragas/ bombachas/calzones	**9.** briefs

sostenedor/sostén/brasier	**10.** bra
fondo entero/refajo	**11.** slip
medias	**12.** stockings
pantimedia	**13.** pantyhose
calcetines/medias	**14.** socks
zapatos	**15.** shoes
zapatillas/tenis	**16.** sneakers
botas	**17.** boots
sandalias	**18.** sandals

[1-14]
A. I can't find my new **pajamas**.
B. Look in the bureau/dresser/closet.

[15-18]
A. Those are very nice **shoes**.
B. Thanks.

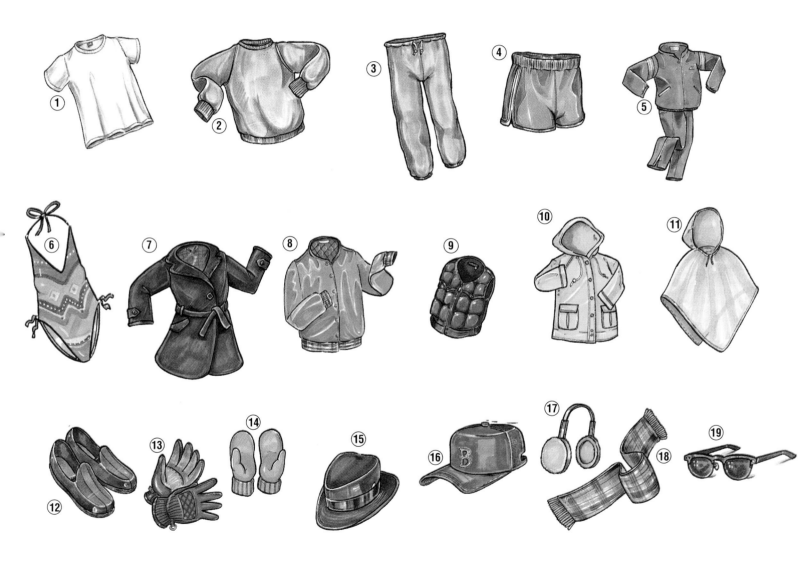

camiseta/playera **1.** tee shirt

sudadera **2.** sweatshirt

pantalones de sudadera **3.** sweat pants

pantalones cortos/
pantaloncillos/calzonas
deportivas/shorts **4.** running shorts

traje para correr **5.** jogging suit

traje de baño/bañador **6.** swimsuit

chaqueta/chamarra **7.** coat

chaqueta/campera/chompa **8.** jacket

chaleco de plumas de ganso **9.** down vest

gabardina/impermeable **10.** raincoat

poncho **11.** poncho

zapatos de goma/
de caucho para la lluvia **12.** rubbers

guantes **13.** gloves

mitones/guantes enteros **14.** mittens

sombrero **15.** hat

gorra de béisbol **16.** baseball cap

orejeras **17.** ear muffs

bufanda **18.** scarf

gafas/anteojos/lentes de sol **19.** sunglasses

A. Excuse me. Is this/Are these your _____?
B. Yes. Thank you.

What do you wear when you exercise?
What do you wear outside when the weather is bad?

anillo/sortija	**1.** ring		llavero	**10.** key ring
anillo/sortija de matrimonio	**2.** wedding band		billetera	**11.** wallet
aretes/pendientes/pantallas	**3.** earrings		monedero	**12.** change purse
collar	**4.** necklace		cartera/bolso/bolsa para damas	**13.** pocketbook/purse
prendedor/broche	**5.** pin			
reloj/reloj de pulsera	**6.** watch		mochila/bolsa para libros	**14.** book bag
pulsera/brazalete	**7.** bracelet		mochila	**15.** backpack
gemelos/mancuernas/yuntas	**8.** cuff links		maletín	**16.** briefcase
cinturón/correa	**9.** belt		paraguas/parasol/sombrilla	**17.** umbrella

A. Oh, no! I think I lost my **ring**!
B. That's too bad!

Do you like to wear jewelry?
What jewelry do you have?
In your country, what do men,
women, and children use to
carry their things?

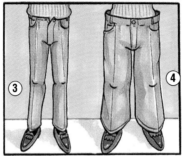

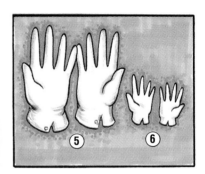

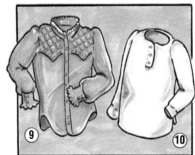

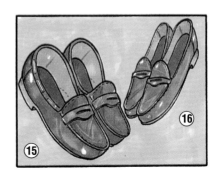

largo(a) – corto(a)	**1–2**	long – short	1–2	Are the sleeves too _____?
estrecho(a) – ancho(a)	**3–4**	tight – loose/baggy	3–4	Are the pants too _____?
grande – chico(a)/pequeño(a)	**5–6**	large/big – small	5–6	Are the gloves too _____?
alto(a) – bajo(a)	**7–8**	high – low	7–8	Are the heels too _____?
adornado(a)– sencillo(a)	**9–10**	fancy – plain	9–10	Is the blouse too _____?
grueso(a) – liviano(a)	**11–12**	heavy – light	11–12	Is the coat too _____?
oscuro(a) – claro(a)	**13–14**	dark – light	13–14	Is the color too _____?
ancho(a) – angosto(a)/ apretado(a)/estrecho(a)	**15–16**	wide – narrow	15–16	Are the shoes too _____?

[1-2]
A. Are the sleeves too **long**?
B. No. They're too **short**.

Describe your favorite clothing.

Name	Value		Written as:
1. penny	one cent	1¢	$ .01
2. nickel	five cents	5¢	$ .05
3. dime	ten cents	10¢	$ .10
4. quarter	twenty-five cents	25¢	$ .25
5. half dollar	fifty cents	50¢	$ .50
6. silver dollar	one dollar		$ 1.00

A. How much is a **penny** worth?
B. A penny is worth **one cent**.

A. Soda costs seventy-five cents.
Do you have enough change?
B. Yes. I have a/two/three _____(s) and . . . .

Name	We sometimes say:	Value	Written as:
1. (one-)dollar bill	a one	one dollar	$ 1.00
2. five-dollar bill	a five	five dollars	$ 5.00
3. ten-dollar bill	a ten	ten dollars	$ 10.00
4. twenty-dollar bill	a twenty	twenty dollars	$ 20.00
5. fifty-dollar bill	a fifty	fifty dollars	$ 50.00
6. (one-)hundred dollar bill	a hundred	one hundred dollars	$100.00

A. Do you have any cash?
B. Yes. I have a **twenty-dollar bill**.

A. Can you change a **five-dollar bill**?
B. Yes. I've got *five* **one-dollar bill**s.

How much do you pay for a loaf of bread? a hamburger? a cup of coffee? a gallon of gas?
Name and describe the coins and currency in your country. What are they worth in U.S. dollars?

chequera/talonario de cheques	**1.**	checkbook
libreta de banco	**2.**	bank book
tarjeta de crédito	**3.**	credit card
la ATH/tarjeta de cajero	**4.**	ATM card
comprobante de depósito	**5.**	deposit slip
comprobante de retiro	**6.**	withdrawal slip
cheque	**7.**	check
giro postal/orden monetaria	**8.**	money order
caja/bóveda	**9.**	vault
cajero/cajera/operador bancario	**10.**	teller
guarda/guardia de seguridad	**11.**	security guard
cajero automático	**12.**	ATM machine/ cash machine
supervisor/ ejecutivo de banco	**13.**	bank officer

[1–4]
A. What are you looking for?
B. My _____.

[5–8]
A. What are you doing?
B. I'm filling out this _____.

[9–13]
A. How many _____s does the State Street Bank have?
B. . . . .

Do you have a bank account? What kind? Where?
Do you have a credit card? When do you use it?

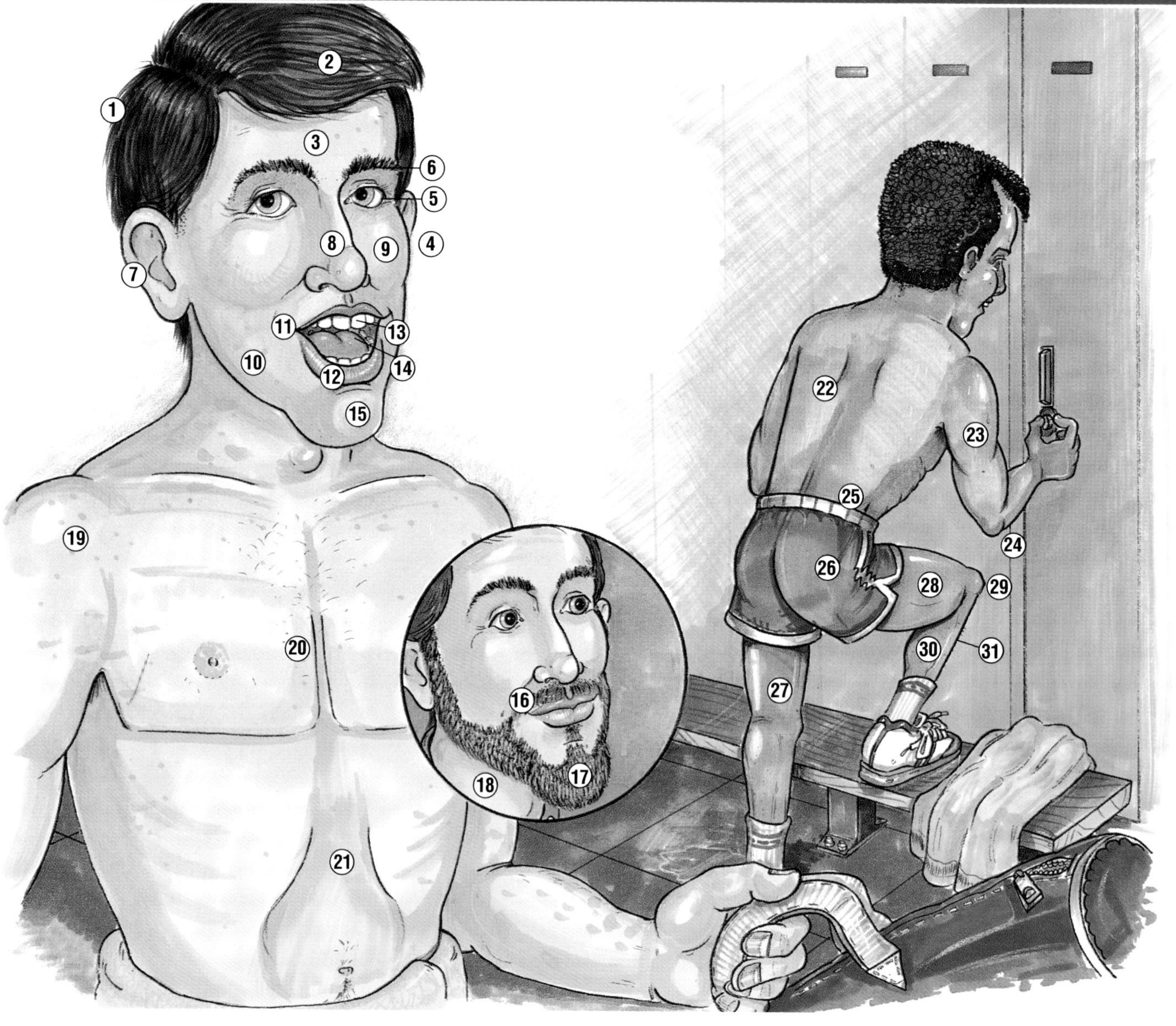
1
2
3
4
5
6
7
8
9
10
11
12
13
14
15
16
17
18
19
20
21
22
23
24
25
26
27
28
29
30
31

cabeza	**1.** head	labio	**12.** lip	brazo	**23.** arm
cabello/pelo	**2.** hair	diente-dientes	**13.** tooth-teeth	codo	**24.** elbow
frente	**3.** forehead	lengua	**14.** tongue	cintura	**25.** waist
cara	**4.** face	mentón/barbilla	**15.** chin	cadera	**26.** hip
ojo	**5.** eye	bigote/mostacho	**16.** mustache	pierna	**27.** leg
ceja	**6.** eyebrow	barba	**17.** beard	muslo	**28.** thigh
oreja/oído	**7.** ear	cuello	**18.** neck	rodilla	**29.** knee
nariz	**8.** nose	hombro	**19.** shoulder	pantorrilla	**30.** calf
mejilla/pómulo	**9.** cheek	pecho	**20.** chest	espinilla	**31.** shin
quijada	**10.** jaw	estómago	**21.** abdomen		
boca	**11.** mouth	espalda	**22.** back		

[1–15, 18–31]

A. My doctor checked my **head** and said everything is okay.

B. I'm glad to hear that.

Describe yourself as completely as you can.

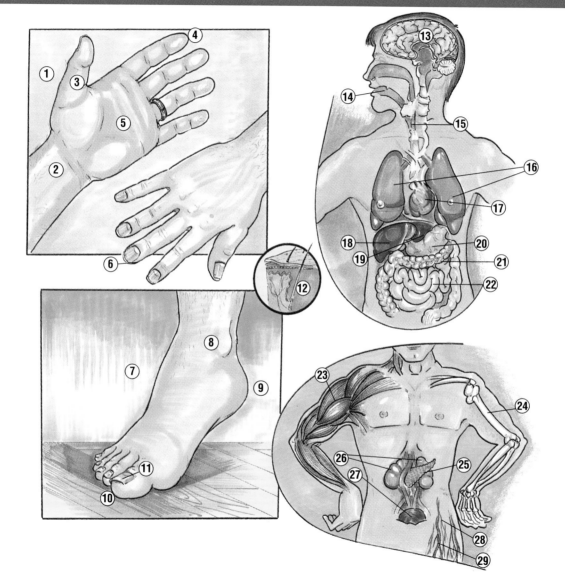

mano	**1.** hand	uña del dedo del pie	**11.** toenail	intestino delgado	**21.** large intestine
muñeca	**2.** wrist	piel	**12.** skin	intestino grueso	**22.** small intestine
pulgar	**3.** thumb	cerebro	**13.** brain	músculos	**23.** muscles
dedo	**4.** finger	garganta	**14.** throat	huesos	**24.** bones
palma	**5.** palm	médula espinal	**15.** spinal cord	páncreas	**25.** pancreas
uña	**6.** fingernail	pulmones	**16.** lungs	riñones	**26.** kidneys
pie	**7.** foot	corazón	**17.** heart	vejiga	**27.** bladder
tobillo	**8.** ankle	hígado	**18.** liver	venas	**28.** veins
talón	**9.** heel	vesícula biliar	**19.** gallbladder	arterias	**29.** arteries
dedo del pie	**10.** toe	estómago	**20.** stomach		

[1–11]
A. What's the matter?
B. I hurt my **hand**.

[12–29]
A. How am I, Doctor?
B. Well, I'm a little concerned about your **lungs**.

Which parts of the body on pages 114–117 are most important in school? at work? when you play your favorite sport?

dolor de cabeza	**1.** headache	infección	**11.** infection
dolor de oído	**2.** earache	salpullido/sarpullido	**12.** rash
dolor de muelas	**3.** toothache	picada/picadura	**13.** insect bite
dolor de estómago	**4.** stomachache	quemadura del sol	**14.** sunburn
dolor de espaldas	**5.** backache	tortícolis	**15.** stiff neck
dolor/ardor de garganta/ garganta inflamada	**6.** sore throat	moqueo	**16.** runny nose
		hemorragia nasal	**17.** bloody nose
fiebre/calentura	**7.** fever	carie	**18.** cavity
gripe/resfriado/catarro/ trancazo	**8.** cold	verruga	**19.** wart
		hipo	**20.** the hiccups
tos	**9.** cough	escalofrío	**21.** the chills
virus	**10.** virus		

Tell about a time you had one of these problems.

A. What's the matter?
B. I have a/an ___[1–19]___ .

A. What's the matter?
B. I have ___[20–21]___ .

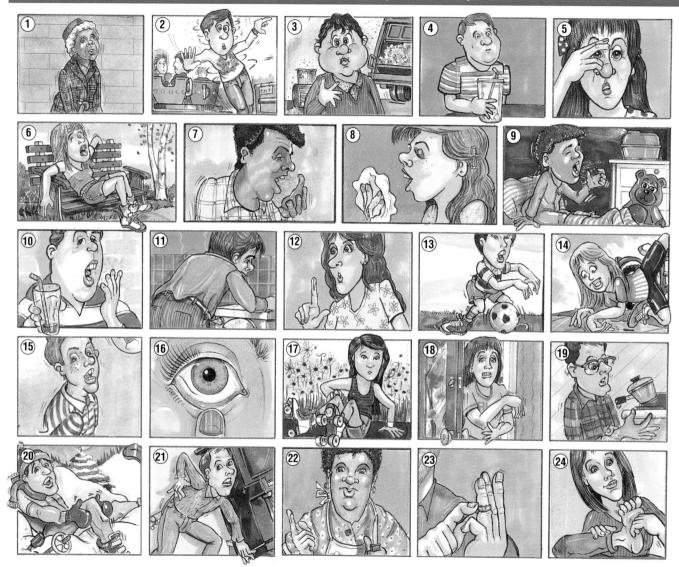

desmayo	**1.** faint		torcerse/retorcerse	**13.** twist
mareo	**2.** dizzy		torcerse	**14.** sprain
náusea	**3.** nauseous		dislocarse	**15.** dislocate
hinchado(a)	**4.** bloated		arañarse	**16.** scratch
congestionado(a)	**5.** congested		rasparse/rasguñarse	**17.** scrape
agotado(a)	**6.** exhausted		magullarse/golpearse	**18.** bruise
toser	**7.** cough		quemarse	**19.** burn
estornudar	**8.** sneeze		romperse	**20.** break–broke
respirar con dificultad	**9.** wheeze		golpearse/lastimarse	**21.** hurt–hurt
eructar	**10.** burp		cortarse	**22.** cut–cut
vomitar/arrojar	**11.** vomit/throw up		inchado	**23.** swollen
sangrar	**12.** bleed		picar	**24.** itchy

A. What's the matter?

B. { I feel __[1–4]__ .
　　I'm __[5–6]__ .
　　I'm __[7–12]__ ing.

A. What's the matter?

B. { I __[13–22]__ ed my . . . .
　　My . . . . is/are __[23–24]__ .

Tell about the last time you didn't feel well. What was the matter?

Tell about a time you hurt yourself. What happened?

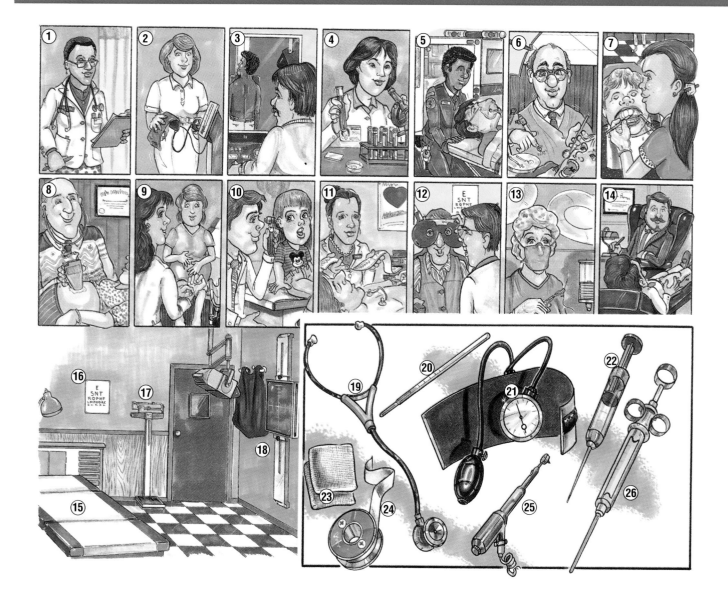

médico/doctor(a) **1.** doctor

enfermera(o) **2.** nurse

radiólogo **3.** X-ray technician

técnico de laboratorio **4.** lab technician

paramédico **5.** EMT/emergency medical technician

dentista **6.** dentist

higienista **7.** hygienist

obstetra **8.** obstetrician

ginecólogo **9.** gynecologist

pediatra **10.** pediatrician

cardiólogo **11.** cardiologist

oculista **12.** optometrist

cirujano **13.** surgeon

psiquiatra **14.** psychiatrist

camilla de examen **15.** examination table

cartilla para medir la visión **16.** eye chart

pesa **17.** scale

máquina de rayos X (equis)/ máquina de radiografías **18.** X-ray machine

estetoscopio **19.** stethoscope

termómetro **20.** thermometer

esfigomanómetro **21.** blood pressure gauge

aguja/jeringa/jeringilla **22.** needle

gasa/venda/vendaje **23.** bandages

esparadrapo **24.** adhesive tape

taladro **25.** drill

anestesia/novocaína **26.** Novocaine

A. What do you do?

B. I'm a/an __[1–14]__ .

A. Please step over here to the __[15–18]__ .

B. Okay.

A. Please hand me the __[19–26]__ .

B. Here you are.

Where do you go for medical care? How often?
Who examines you? What does he/she do?

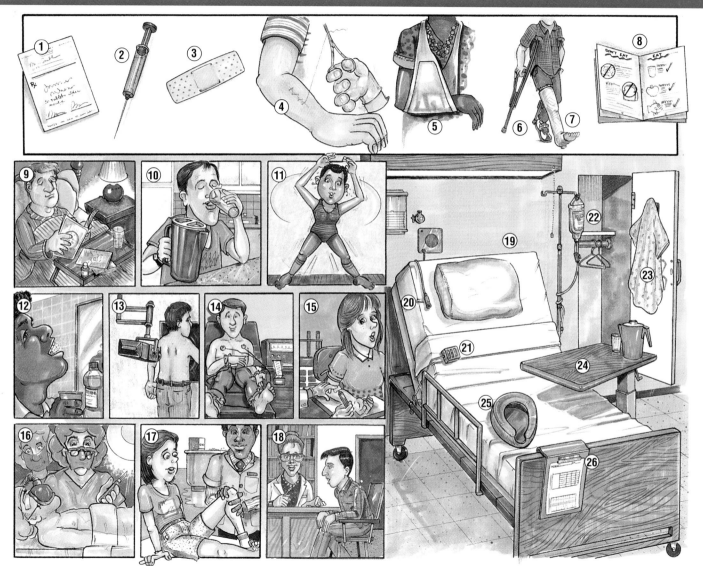

receta médica	**1.** prescription	análisis/pruebas	**14.** tests
inyección	**2.** injection	análsis/pruebas de sangre	**15.** blood tests
curita/tirita/parche/venda	**3.** bandaid	operación	**16.** surgery
puntos	**4.** stitches	fisioterapia	**17.** physical therapy
cabestrillo	**5.** sling	asesoramiento médico	**18.** counseling
muletas	**6.** crutches	cama de hospital	**19.** hospital bed
yeso/enyesado/escayola	**7.** cast	timbre	**20.** call button
dieta/régimen	**8.** diet	control de la cama	**21.** bed control
guardar cama	**9.** rest in bed	venoclisis/intravenosa	**22.** I.V.
tomar líquidos	**10.** drink fluids	bata de hospital	**23.** hospital gown
hacer ejercicios	**11.** exercise	mesa	**24.** bed table
hacer gárgaras	**12.** gargle	paleta/cuña	**25.** bed pan
radiografías/rayos X (equis)	**13.** X-rays	cuadrícula/hoja clínica	**26.** medical chart

A. What did the doctor do?
B. She/He gave me (a/an) _[1–8]_ .

A. What did the doctor say?
B. { I need to _[9–12]_ .
    { I need _[13–18]_ .

A. This is your _[19–26]_ .
B. I see.

When did you have your last medical checkup?
What did the doctor say?

Tell about a time you were in the hospital.

aspirina	**1.** aspirin
pastillas/píldoras para la gripe	**2.** cold tablets
vitaminas	**3.** vitamins
jarabe para la tos	**4.** cough syrup
pastillas para la tos	**5.** cough drops
pastillas para la garganta	**6.** throat lozenges
antiácido/tabletas para la acidez estomacal	**7.** antacid tablets
descongestionante nasal (en atomizador)	**8.** decongestant spray/ nasal spray
gota para los ojos	**9.** eye drops
ungüento	**10.** ointment

crema/pomada	**11.** creme
loción	**12.** lotion
parche caliente	**13.** heating pad
bolsa de hielo	**14.** ice pack
silla de ruedas	**15.** wheelchair
píldora	**16.** pill
pastilla/tableta	**17.** tablet
cápsula	**18.** capsule
cápsula comprimida/capeleta	**19.** caplet
cucharadita	**20.** teaspoon
cucharada	**21.** tablespoon

A. What did the doctor say?

B. { I need to take ___[1–4]___ .
I need to use (a/an) ___[5–15]___ .

A. What's the dosage?

B. One ___[16–21]___ , every three hours.

What medicines do you take or use?
For what ailments?

Describe any medical treatments or medicines in your country that are different from the ones in these lessons.

carta	**1.** letter	giro postal/orden monetaria	**15.** money order	
tarjeta postal	**2.** postcard	forma: cambio de dirección	**16.** change-of-address form	
aerograma	**3.** aerogramme	solicitud para servicio selectivo	**17.** selective service registration form	
paquete postal	**4.** package	sobre	**18.** envelope	
primera clase	**5.** first class	dirección	**19.** address	
correo aéreo	**6.** air mail	código/área postal	**20.** zip code	
paquete postal	**7.** parcel post	señas del remitente	**21.** return address	
tercera clase	**8.** book rate	estampilla	**22.** stamp	
certificado	**9.** registered mail	ventanilla	**23.** window	
entrega inmediata	**10.** express mail	empleado de correos	**24.** postal worker/postal clerk	
estampilla/sello	**11.** stamp	máquinilla de sellos	**25.** stamp machine	
pliego de sellos	**12.** sheet of stamps	camión de correos	**26.** mail truck	
rollo de sellos	**13.** roll of stamps	buzón	**27.** mailbox	
carterita de sellos	**14.** book of stamps	cartero(a)	**28.** letter carrier	

A. Where are you going?
B. To the post office. I have to mail a/an [1–4] .

A. How do you want to send it?
B. [5–10] , please.

A. Next!
B. I'd like a [11–17] , please.
A. Here you are.

A. I'll mail this letter for you.
B. Thanks.
A. Oops! You forgot the [19–22] !

Describe the post office you use: How many windows are there? Is there a stamp machine? Are the postal workers friendly?

Tell about the postal system in your country.

bibliotecario(a)	**1.** librarian	atlas	**7.** atlas
recepción/ mostrador de chequeo	**2.** checkout desk	enciclopedia	**8.** encyclopedia
		diccionario	**9.** dictionary
ayudante	**3.** library assistant	periódico	**10.** newspaper
catálogo/tarjetero/fichero	**4.** card catalog	revista	**11.** magazine
estantería/librero(a)/ anaqueles/tablillas	**5.** shelves	ficha/tarjeta	**12.** call card
información	**6.** information desk	carnet/tarjeta de identificación	**13.** library card

[1–11]

A. Excuse me. Where's/Where are the _____(s)?
B. Over there.

Tell about the library you go to. Describe how to use the library.

oficina	**1.** office		auditorio	**13.** auditorium
enfermería	**2.** nurse's office		campo de juego	**14.** field
consejería	**3.** guidance office		gradería/gradas/bancas	**15.** bleachers
cafetería	**4.** cafeteria		pista/cancha	**16.** track
dirección	**5.** principal's office		director(a)	**17.** principal
salón/sala de clases/aula	**6.** classroom		subdirector(a)	**18.** assistant principal
			enfermero(a)	**19.** school nurse
casillero	**7.** locker		consejero(a)	**20.** guidance counselor
laboratorio de lenguas	**8.** language lab		maestro(a) de manejo/ de conducir	**21.** driver's ed instructor
laboratorio de química	**9.** chemistry lab		maestro(a)	**22.** teacher
salón/sala de profesores	**10.** teachers' lounge		entrenador(a)	**23.** coach
gimnasio	**11.** gym		portero(a)/conserje	**24.** custodian
vestidor/vestidores	**12.** locker room			

A. Where are you going?
B. I'm going to the ___[1–16]___ .*
A. Do you have a hall pass?
B. Yes. Here it is.

*With 6 and 7, use: I'm going to my _____.

A. Who's that?
B. That's the new ___[17–24]___ .

Describe the school where you study English. Tell about the rooms, offices, and people.

Tell about differences between schools in the United States and in your country.

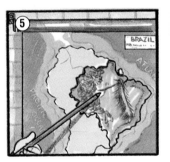

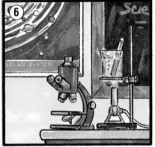

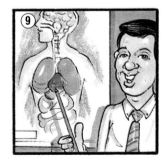

matemáticas	**1.** math	español	**7.** Spanish
álgebra	**2.** algebra	economía doméstica	**8.** home economics
inglés	**3.** English	higiene	**9.** health
historia	**4.** history	curso de manejo	**10.** driver's ed
geografía	**5.** geography	arte	**11.** art
ciencias	**6.** science	música	**12.** music

A. What do you have next period?
B. _____. How about you?
A. _____.

What is/was your favorite subject in school? Why?

banda	**1.** band		periódico estudiantil	**6.** school newspaper
orquesta	**2.** orchestra		anuario	**7.** yearbook
coro	**3.** choir		revista literaria	**8.** literary magazine
drama/teatro	**4.** drama		asociación de estudiantes	**9.** student government
fútbol americano	**5.** football			

A. Are you going home right after school?

B. { No. I have __[1–5]__ practice.
   { No. I have a __[6–9]__ meeting.

What extracurricular activities do/did you participate in?

contable/contador **1.** accountant

actor **2.** actor

actriz **3.** actress

artista **4.** artist

montador(a) **5.** assembler

barbero(a) **6.** barber

albañil **7.** bricklayer

busero(a)/conductor(a)/ **8.** bus driver
chofer de autobús

carnicero(a) **9.** butcher

carpintero(a) **10.** carpenter

cajero(a) **11.** cashier

A. What do you do?
B. I'm an **accountant**.

Which of these occupations do you think is the most interesting? Why?

chef/cocinero(a)	**1.**	chef/cook
programador(a)	**2.**	computer programmer
obrero(a)	**3.**	construction worker
portero(a)/conserje	**4.**	custodian/janitor
repartidor	**5.**	delivery person
electricista	**6.**	electrician
granjero/agricultor/ hacendado	**7.**	farmer

pescador	**8.**	fisherman
maestro de obras/capataz	**9.**	foreman
jardinero(a)	**10.**	gardener
peluquero(a)	**11.**	hairdresser
ama de casa	**12.**	housekeeper

A. What do you do?
B. I'm a **chef**.

Which of these occupations do you think is the most difficult? Why?

abogado(a)	**1.** lawyer	policía	**7.** police officer
mecánico(a)	**2.** mechanic	mecánico(a)	**8.** repairperson
mensajero	**3.** messenger	periodista/reportero(a)	**9.** reporter
pintor(a)	**4.** painter	vendedor(a)	**10.** salesperson
boticario/farmacéutico(a)/ farmacista	**5.** pharmacist	empleado del departamento de salubridad	**11.** sanitation worker
plomero(a)	**6.** plumber		

A. What's your occupation?
B. I'm a **lawyer**.
A. A **lawyer**?
B. Yes. That's right.

Which of these occupations do you think is the most important? Why?

científico(a)	**1.** scientist	camionero(a)	**7.** truck driver
costurero(a)	**2.** seamstress	veterinario(a)	**8.** veterinarian
secretario(a)	**3.** secretary	camarero/mesero	**9.** waiter
guarda/guardia de seguridad	**4.** security guard	camarera/mesera	**10.** waitress
empleado (del depósito)	**5.** stock clerk	soldador(a)	**11.** welder
taxista	**6.** taxi driver		

A. What do you do?
B. I'm a **scientist**. How about you?
A. I'm a **security guard**.

Do you work? What's your occupation? What are the occupations of the people in your family?

actuar **1.** act

armar componentes/ **2.** assemble
montar componentes *components*

hacer cosas/ **3.** build *things/*
construir cosas construct *things*

limpiar **4.** clean

cocinar **5.** cook

repartir pizzas **6.** deliver *pizzas*

conducir/manejar **7.** drive a *truck*
un camión

archivar **8.** file

sembrar vegetales **9.** grow *vegetables*

vigilar edificios/ **10.** guard *buildings*
cuidar edificios

cortar el césped/la **11.** mow *lawns*
grama/el zacate

A. Can you **act**?
B. Yes, I can.

Can you do any of these work activities? Which ones?

manejar/operar **1.** operate *equipment*
herramientas/máquinas
pintar **2.** paint
tocar *el piano* **3.** play the *piano*
arreglar/componer *cosas* **4.** repair *things*/fix *things*
vender *autos/carros* **5.** sell *cars*
servir *comida* **6.** serve *food*

coser **7.** sew
cantar **8.** sing
enseñar **9.** teach
escribir *a máquina* **10.** type
lavar *platos* **11.** wash *dishes*
escribir **12.** write

A. Do you know how to **operate** *equipment*?
B. Yes, I do.

Tell about your work abilities. What can you do?

reloj marcador	**1.** time clock		cinta/correa	**14.** conveyor belt
tarjetas (de asistencia)	**2.** time cards		transportadora	
cuarto de suministros	**3.** supply room		almacén/depósito	**15.** warehouse
anteojos/lentes protectores/	**4.** safety glasses		portacarga	**16.** forklift
gafas protectoras			montacarga	**17.** freight elevator
máscaras	**5.** masks		máquina dispensadora/	**18.** vending machine
cadena/línea de montaje	**6.** (assembly) line		vendedora automática	
obrero/operario	**7.** worker		buzón de sugerencias	**19.** suggestion box
lugar/posición de trabajo	**8.** work station		cafetería	**20.** cafeteria
capataz	**9.** foreman		sección de envíos	**21.** shipping department
máquina	**10.** machine		carrito manual	**22.** hand truck
palanca	**11.** lever		muelle de carga	**23.** loading dock
extinguidor de fuego/extintor	**12.** fire extinguisher		oficina de pagos	**24.** payroll office
maletín de primeros auxilios	**13.** first-aid kit		oficina de personal	**25.** personnel office

A. Excuse me. I'm a new employee.
   Where's/Where are the _____?
B. Next to/Near/In/On the _____.

A. Where's Fred?
B. He's in/on/at/next to/near
   the _____.

Are there any factories where you live?
What kind? What are the working conditions?

What products do factories in your country
produce?

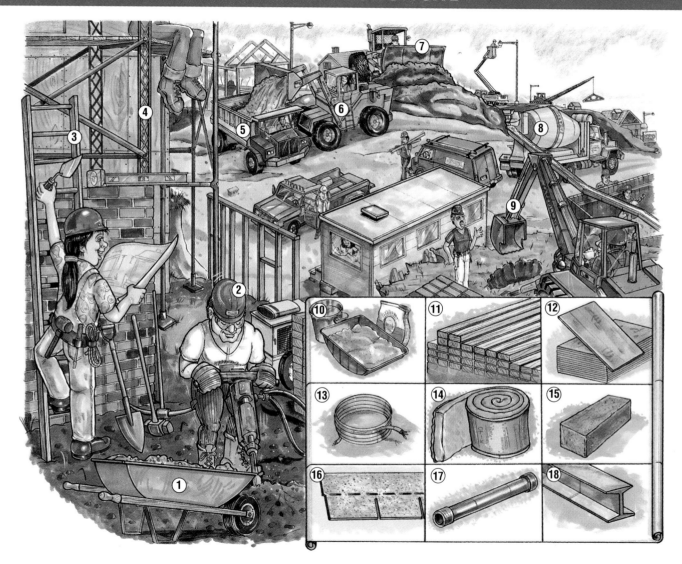

Español	English	Español	English
carretilla	1. wheelbarrow	cemento	10. cement
casco de construcción	2. helmet	madera	11. wood/lumber
escalera	3. ladder	madera contrachapeada/ madera prensada	12. plywood
andamio	4. scaffolding		
volquete/camión de volquete/de volteo	5. dump truck	alambre	13. wire
		fibra aisladora	14. insulation
cargadora/pala cargadora	6. front-end loader	ladrillo	15. brick
excavadora/pala excavadora/ buldozer	7. bulldozer	teja	16. shingle
		tubería/tubo/pipa/paipa	17. pipe
hormigonera/concretera/ mezcladora de cemento	8. cement mixer	viga	18. girder/beam
tractor excavador/pala excavadora	9. backhoe		

A. Could you get me that/those __[1–3]__ ?
B. Sure.

A. Watch out for that __[4–9]__ !
B. Oh! Thanks for the warning!

A. Are we going to have enough __[10–14]__ / __[15–18]__ s to finish the job?
B. I think so.

What building materials is your home made of?
Describe a construction site near your home or school.

luz delantera/faro	1.	headlight	llanta de repuesto	15.	spare tire
parachoques/defensa	2.	bumper	señales de peligro	16.	flare
llanta/neumático/goma	3.	tire	cables de conexión/reactivadores	17.	jumper cables
toldo/capó del motor	4.	hood	motor	18.	engine
parabrisas	5.	windshield	bujías	19.	spark plugs
limpiaparabrisas	6.	windshield wipers	carburador	20.	carburetor
antena	7.	antenna	batería	21.	battery
descongelador de vidrio trasero	8.	rear defroster	radiador	22.	radiator
			banda/correa del ventilador	23.	fan belt
maletero/baúl/cajuela	9.	trunk	gasolinera/bomba/estación de gasolina	24.	service station/gas station
luz (trasera)	10.	taillight			
placa de matrícula/tablilla	11.	license plate	bomba de aire	25.	air pump
			mecánico(a)	26.	mechanic
tubo de escape	12.	tailpipe	ayudante/asistente	27.	attendant
silenciador	13.	muffler	surtidor/bomba/pompa de gasolina	28.	gas pump
gato(a)	14.	jack			

[1, 2, 4–8, 12, 13, 22, 23]

A. What's the matter with your car?

B. The _____(s) is/are broken.

[1, 3, 6, 7, 10, 19–21, 23]

A. Can I help you?

B. Yes. I need to replace a/the _____(s).

Do you own a car?
Describe it.

visera	**1.** visor
espejo retrovisor	**2.** rearview mirror
tablero/panel de instrumentos/de mandos	**3.** dashboard
velocímetro	**4.** speedometer
palanca de direccionales	**5.** turn signal
eje	**6.** steering column
bolsa de aire	**7.** air bag
claxón/bocina/pito	**8.** horn
encendido	**9.** ignition
radio	**10.** radio
guantera/gavetera	**11.** glove compartment
freno de emergencia	**12.** emergency brake
freno	**13.** brake
acelerador	**14.** accelerator/gas pedal
engranaje de cambios	**15.** gearshift
mando de transmisión automática	**16.** automatic transmission
embrague/clutch	**17.** clutch
palanca/mando de cambios	**18.** stickshift
transmisión manual	**19.** manual transmission
cinturón de seguridad	**20.** shoulder harness
cinturón de seguridad	**21.** seat belt

A. The car has a very nice **visor**.
B. I see.

Describe the interior of a car you are familiar with.

tren	**A. train**
estación (del tren)	1. train station
taquilla/ventanilla	2. ticket window
horario	3. schedule/timetable
tren	4. train
riel	5. track
pasajero	6. passenger
cobrador(a)/inspector(a)	7. conductor
equipaje	8. luggage/baggage
maletero(a)	9. porter
locomotora	10. engine
maquinista/conductor(a)	11. engineer
coche de pasajeros	12. passenger car
coche cama	13. sleeper
coche restaurante	14. dining car
autobús/bus	**B. bus**
autobús/bus/	15. bus
chofer/conductor(a)	16. bus driver

estación de autobuses	17. bus station
mostrador de boletos	18. ticket counter
autobús/bus	**C. local bus**
paradero de autobuses	19. bus stop
pasajero	20. rider/passenger
subterráneo/metro	**D. subway**
estación	21. subway station
subterráneo/metro	22. subway
caja/cajilla de fichas	23. token booth
contador de entrada	24. turnstile
ficha/token	25. token
contraseña	26. fare card
máquina para la contraseña	27. fare card machine
taxi	**E. taxi**
parada de taxis/piquera	28. taxi stand
taxi	29. taxi/cab
medidor/marcador	30. meter
taxista/chofer de taxi	31. cab driver/taxi driver

[A–E]

A. How are you going to get there?

B. { I'm going to take the __[A–D]__.
   I'm going to take a __[E]__.

[1–5, 7–19, 21–24, 27, 28]

A. Excuse me. Where's the _____?

B. Over there.

How do you get to school or work?

Describe public transportation where you live.

In your country, can you travel far by train or by bus? Where can you go? Describe the buses and trains.

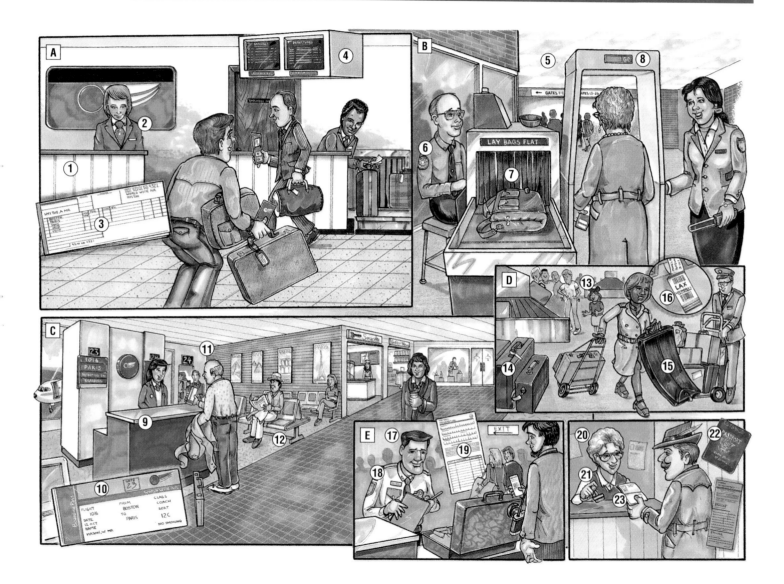

Registro (de pasajeros) **A. Check-In**

mostrador de pasajes **1.** ticket counter

expendedor de pasajes **2.** ticket agent

pasaje/boleto/billete **3.** ticket

control de llegadas y **4.** arrival and departure
salidas   monitor

Seguridad **B. Security**

control de seguridad **5.** security checkpoint

guarda de seguridad **6.** security guard

máquina de rayos X **7.** X-ray machine

detector de metales **8.** metal detector

Area de entradas y salidas **C. The Gate**

mostrador de factura/ **9.** check-in counter
registro/chequeo

pase de abordaje **10.** boarding pass

puerta/sala **11.** gate

sala de espera **12.** waiting area

Reclamo de equipaje **D. Baggage Claim**

área de reclamo/ **13.** baggage claim area
de retiro de equipaje

maleta **14.** suitcase

bolsa para trajes **15.** garment bag

boleto de factura **16.** baggage claim check
del equipaje

Emigración y Aduana **E. Customs and Immigration**

aduana **17.** customs

oficial de aduana **18.** customs officer

tarjeta de declaración **19.** customs declaration form
de aduana

emigración/inmigración **20.** immigration

empleado de **21.** immigration officer
emigración/inmigración

pasaporte **22.** passport

visa **23.** visa

[1, 2, 4–9, 11–13, 17, 18, 20, 21]

A. Excuse me. Where's the _____?*

B. Right over there.

*With 17 and 20, use: Excuse me. Where's _____?

[3, 10, 14–16, 19, 22, 23]

A. Oh, no! I lost my _____!

B. I'll help you look for it.

Describe an airport you are familiar with.   Tell about a time you went through Customs and Immigration.

Estado del tiempo	**A.**	**Weather**
soleado	**1.**	sunny
nublado	**2.**	cloudy
despejado	**3.**	clear
brumoso/con bruma/con calina	**4.**	hazy
con niebla/con neblina	**5.**	foggy
con viento/ventoso	**6.**	windy
húmedo/pegajoso/bochornoso	**7.**	humid/muggy
lloviendo	**8.**	raining
lloviznando	**9.**	drizzling
nevando	**10.**	snowing
granizando	**11.**	hailing
callisqueando/helando	**12.**	sleeting
relámpago(s)/relampagueando	**13.**	lightning
tormenta de truenos	**14.**	thunderstorm
tormenta de nieve	**15.**	snowstorm
huracán/tifón	**16.**	hurricane/typhoon
tornado/torbellino	**17.**	tornado
Temperatura ambiental	**B.**	**Temperature**
termómetro	**18.**	thermometer
Farenheit	**19.**	Fahrenheit
Centígrado/Celcius	**20.**	Centigrade/Celsius
caliente	**21.**	hot
caluroso/cálido	**22.**	warm
fresco	**23.**	cool
frío	**24.**	cold
helado	**25.**	freezing
Estaciones	**C.**	**Seasons**
verano	**26.**	summer
otoño	**27.**	fall/autumn
invierno	**28.**	winter
primavera	**29.**	spring

A. What's the weather like?
B. It's __[1–12]__ .

A. What's the weather forecast?
B. There's going to be __[13]__ /a __[14–17]__ .

A. How's the weather?
B. It's __[21–25]__ .
A. What's the temperature?
B. It's . . . . degrees __[19,20]__ .

Describe the seasons where you live.
Tell about the weather and the temperature.

What's your favorite season?
Why?

trotar	**1.** jogging		nadar	**9.** swimming	
correr	**2.** running		pescar/ir de pesca	**10.** fishing	
andar	**3.** walking		jugar tenis	**11.** tennis	
patinar	**4.** roller skating		béisbol	**12.** baseball	
montar bicicleta	**5.** bicycling		fútbol americano	**13.** football	
esquiar/hacer esquí alpino	**6.** skiing		baloncesto/básquetbol	**14.** basketball	
patinar sobre hielo	**7.** skating		fútbol/fútbol soccer/balompié	**15.** soccer	
navegar en velero	**8.** sailing				

A. What do you like to do in your free time?

B. { I like to go   [1–10] .
   { I like to play [11–15] .

Do you do any of these activities? Which ones? Which are popular in your country?

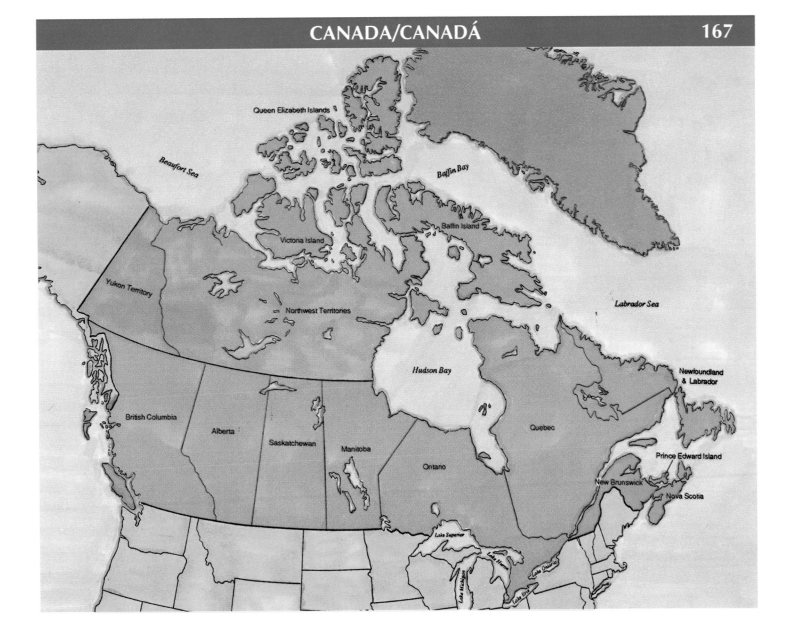

Queen Elizabeth Islands

Beaufort Sea

Baffin Bay

Victoria Island

Baffin Island

Labrador Sea

Yukon Territory

Northwest Territories

Hudson Bay

Newfoundland & Labrador

British Columbia

Alberta

Saskatchewan

Manitoba

Quebec

Ontario

Prince Edward Island

New Brunswick

Nova Scotia

Lake Superior

Lake Michigan

Lake Huron

Lake Ontario

Lake Erie

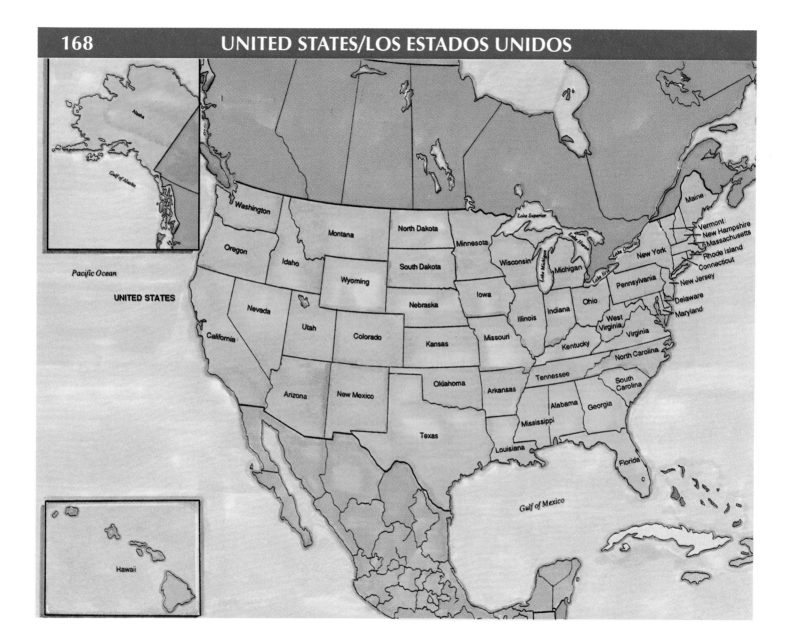

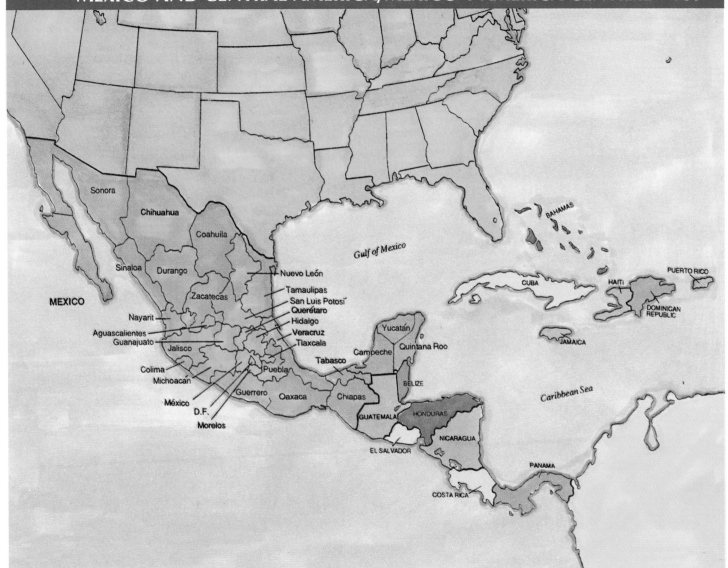

Sonora

Chihuahua

Coahuila

Gulf of Mexico

BAHAMAS

Sinaloa

Durango

Nuevo León

PUERTO RICO

MEXICO

Zacatecas

Tamaulipas

San Luis Potosí

Querétaro

Hidalgo

Veracruz

Tlaxcala

CUBA

HAITI

DOMINICAN
REPUBLIC

Nayarit

Aguascalientes

Guanajuato

Jalisco

Yucatán

JAMAICA

Campeche

Quintana Roo

Colima

Michoacan

Puebla

Tabasco

México

D.F.

Morelos

Guerrero

Oaxaca

Chiapas

BELIZE

Caribbean Sea

GUATEMALA

HONDURAS

EL SALVADOR

NICARAGUA

PANAMA

COSTA RICA

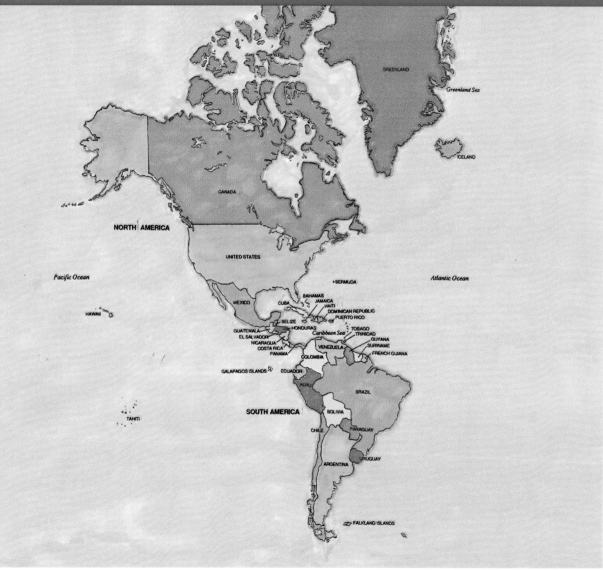

NORTH AMERICA

SOUTH AMERICA

CANADA

UNITED STATES

MÉXICO

GREENLAND

Greenland Sea

ICELAND

Pacific Ocean

Atlantic Ocean

• BERMUDA

HAWAII

BAHAMAS
CUBA
JAMAICA
HAITI
DOMINICAN REPUBLIC
PUERTO RICO

BELIZE
GUATEMALA
HONDURAS
EL SALVADOR
NICARAGUA
COSTA RICA
PANAMA

Caribbean Sea

TOBAGO
TRINIDAD
GUYANA
SURINAME
FRENCH GUIANA

VENEZUELA
COLOMBIA

GALAPAGOS ISLANDS
ECUADOR

PERU
BRAZIL
BOLIVIA
CHILE
PARAGUAY
ARGENTINA
URUGUAY

TAHITI

FALKLAND ISLANDS

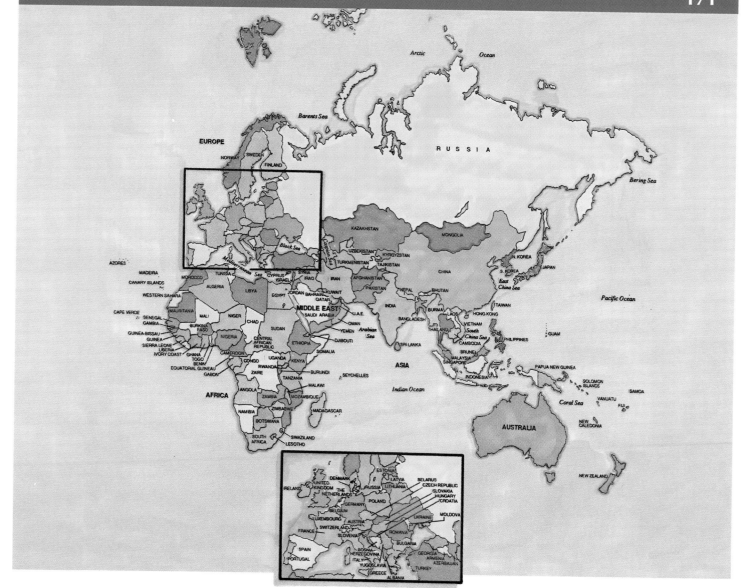

teaspoon
tsp.

cucharadita
cdta.

tablespoon
Tbsp.

cucharada
cda.

1 (fluid) ounce
1 fl. oz.

una onza
1 oz. líquida

cup
8 fl. ozs.

una taza
8 ozs. líquidas

pint
pt.
16 fl. ozs.

una pinta
16 ozs. líquidas

quart
qt.
32 fl. ozs.

un cuarto
32 ozs. líquidas

gallon
gal.
128 fl. ozs.

un galón
128 ozs. líquidas

an ounce

oz.

una onza
1 oz.

a quarter
of a pound
¼ lb.
4 ozs.

un cuarto de libra
1/4 lb.
4 ozs.

half a pound

½ lb.
8 ozs.

media libra
1/2 lb.
8 ozs.

three-quarters
of a pound
¾ lb.
12 ozs.

tres cuartos de libra
3/4 lb.
12 ozs.

a pound

lb.
16 ozs.

una libra
1 lb.
16 ozs.

El número en negritas indica la página donde aparece la palabra; el número que sigue indica donde se encuentra la palabra en la ilustración y en la lista de palabras. Por ejemplo, "esposa" **5-1** indica que la palabra *esposa* está en la página 5 y es la primera entrada.

iguales **50**
imperdibles **33**-9
impermeable **105**-10
inchado **121**-23
infección **119**-11
información **131**-6
inglés **135**-3
inmigración **161**-20
inodoro **35**-2
inspector(a) **159**-7
intercomunicador **31**-2
intestino delgado **117**-21
intestino grueso **117**-22
intravenosa **125**-22
invierno **163**-28
inyección **125**-2
ir de pesca **165**-10

jabón **35**-18, **83**-16
jabón para la lavadora de platos **29**-2
jabón líquido para lavar platos **29**-3
jamón **85**-5
jarabe para la tos **127**-4
jardinero(a) **45**-8, **141**-10
jarra **23**-8
jarrita para la crema **23**-21
jarrita para la leche **23**-21
jeans **101**-4
jeringa **123**-22
jeringuilla **123**-22
jersey **101**-8
joven **69**-29
joyas **106**
joyero **27**-17
judías verdes **79**-14
juego de cubiertos **25**
jugar **11**-15

jugar baloncesto **11**-16
jugar básquetbol **11**-16
jugar tenis **165**-11
jugo **83**-21
jugo de china **81**-4
jugo de naranja **81**-4
juguetería **63**-8
juzado **65**-4

kiwi **77**-8
Kleenex **83**-13

labio **115**-12
laboratorio de lenguas **133**-8
laboratorio de química **133**-9
ladrillo **153**-15
lámpara **21**-6, **47**-10
lámpara de mesa **21**-6
lámpara de techo **23**-5
lamparilla **31**-6
lamparita **31**-6
langosta **85**-13
langostinos **85**-10
lápiz **13**-6
lápiz de labio **37**-23
largo(a) **69**-3, **109**-1
lastimarse (me lastimé) **121**-21
lata **89**-6
lata para harina, azúcar, té o sal **29**-18
lavabo **35**-15
lavadora **39**-8
lavadora de platos **29**-1
lavamanos **35**-15
lavamático **61**-2
lavandería **43**-13, **61**-2

lavandería en seco **57**-8
lavaplatos **29**-1, **97**-7
lavar (lavo) platos **11**-5, **149**-11
lavar la ropa **11**-6
lavarme la cara **9**-7
lavarme los dientes **9**-3
lavavajillas **97**-7
lea(n) la página ocho **15**-7
leche **81**-1, **95**-18
leche búlgara **81**-11
leche con chocolate **81**-2
lechera **23**-21
lechuga **79**-1
leer **11**-14
lengua **115**-14
lentes de sol **105**-19
lentes protectores **151**-4
lento(a) **69**-16
letrero con el nombre de la calle **67**-4
levantarse **9**-1
levánte(n)se **15**-1
libra **91**-10, **172**
librería **57**-4
librero(a) **13**-28, **21**-27, **131**-5
libreta **13**-11
libreta de banco **113**-2
libro **13**-10
libro de recetas de cocina **29**-25
libro de texto **13**-10
lija **47**-14
lima **77**-20
limón (amarillo) **77**-19
limón verde **77**-20
limonada **95**-13
limpiaparabrisas **155**-6

limpiar (limpio) **147**-4
limpiar el apartamento **11**-1
limpiar las casa **11**-1
limpio(a) **71**-9
línea de montage **151**-6
línea de seguridad **67**-11
linterna **47**-10
liso(a) **69**-19, **71**-5
litro **91**-9
liviano(a) **69**-12, **109**-12
loción **127**-12
loción para niños **33**-2
locomotora **159**-10
lucecita **31**-6
lugar de trabajo **151**-8
luz delantera **155**-1
luz (trasera) **155**-10

llanta **95**-1, **155**-3
llanta de repuesta **155**-15
llave **29**-4, **35**-16, 22
llave inglesa **47**-3, 5
llave para tuercas **47**-3
llavero **107**-10
lleno(a) **71**-25
lloviendo **163**-8
lloviznando **163**-9

madera **153**-11
madera contrachapeada **153**-12
madera prensada **153**-12
madre **5**-3
maestro(a) **13**-1, **133**-22
maestro(a) de conducir **133**-21
maestro(a) de manejo **133**-21
maestro de obras **141**-9

magullarse (me maguillé) **121**-18
maíz **79**-4
malestar **118**
maleta **161**-14
maletero **155**-9, **159**-9
maletín **107**-16
maletín de primeros auxilios **151**-13
malo(a)(s) **69**-32
mamá **5**-3
mamadera **33**-14, 15
mancuernas **107**-8
mandarina **77**-22
mando de cambios **157**-18
mando de transmisión automática **157**-16
manejar (manejo) *herramientas, máquinas* **149**-1
manejar (manejo) un *camión* **147**-7
mango **77**-10
manguera **47**-23
mano **117**-1
manojo **89**-5
manta **27**-6
manta eléctrica **27**-7
mantacarga **151**-17
mantel **23**-11
mantelito individual **29**-31
mantequilla **81**-6
mantequillera **23**-17
manzana **77**-1
mapa **13**-25
maquillaje **37**-25
maquillarse **9**-8
máquina **151**-10

paipa **153**-17
pala **47**-22
pala cargadora **153**-6
pala excavadora **153**-7, 9
palanca **151**-11
palanca de cambios **157**-18
palanca de direccionales **157**-5
paleta **125**-25
palillos de algodón **33**-8
palitos de algodón **33**-8
palma **117**-5
pan **83**-30
panadería **57**-1
páncreas **117**-25
panecillo **95**-5
panecillo dulce **95**-2
panecillo(s) **83**-31, **95**-5
panel de instrumentos **157**-3
panel de mandos **157**-3
paño **29**-12
pantaletas **103**-9
pantalla **13**-31, **21**-7
pantallas **107**-3
pantaloncillos **103**-6, **105**-4
pantaloncillos boxer **103**-7
pantalones **101**-3
pantalones cortos **101**-7, **105**-4
pantalones de dril **101**-4
pantalones de mezclila **101**-4
pantalones de sudadera **105**-3
panti bikini **103**-8

pantimedia **103**-13
pantis **103**-9
pantorilla **115**-30
pantuflas **103**-4
pañales de algodón **33**-11
pañales de tela **33**-11
pañales desechables **33**-10
paño de cocina **29**-12
pañuelos de papel **83**-13
papa **79**-25
papá **5**-4
papa dulce **79**-27
papaya **77**-9
papel **13**-12
papel absorbente **39**-10
papel cuadriculado **13**-13
papel higiénico **35**-5, **83**-15
papel toalla **39**-10, **83**-17
papillas **33**-6
paquete **91**-3
paquete postal **129**-4, 7
parabrisas **155**-5
parachoques **155**-2
parada de autobuses (de guaguas) **65**-11
parada de taxis **67**-1, **159**-28
paradero de autobuses (de guaguas) **65**-11, **159**-19
paraguas **107**-17
paramédico **123**-5
parasol **107**-17
parche **125**-3
parche antirresbalón **35**-27
parche caliente **127**-13
pardo **99**-11
pared **21**-13

parque **61**-8
parquímetro **65**-16
parrilla **41**-19
pasaje **161**-3
pasajero **159**-6, 20
pasaporte **161**-22
pasar la aspiradora **11**-4
pase de abordaje **161**-10
pase(n) *el examen* **17**-7
pase(n) *la prueba* **17**-7
pasear al perro **11**-10
pasitas **77**-27
paso peatonal **67**-11
pasta **83**-25
pasta de dientes **37**-15
pasta lustradora para zapatos **37**-24
pastelería **57**-1
pasteles **95**-4
pastilla **127**-17
pastillas para la garganta **127**-6
pastillas para la gripe **127**-2
pastillas para la tos **127**-5
pastinaca **79**-36
patata **79**-25
patinar **165**-4
partinar sobre hielo **165**-7
patio **41**-17
pavo **85**-8
peatón **67**-12
pecho **115**-20
pediatra **123**-10
pegajoso **163**-7
peinarme el cabello **9**-10
peine **37**-2
peinilla **37**-2

pele(a) **93**-5
pelo **115**-2
peluche **31**-1, 13
peluquería **59**-6
peluquero(a) **141**-11
pendientes **107**-3
pepinillo **79**-19
pepino **79**-19
pequeño(a) **69**-6, **109**-6
pera **77**-3
perfume **37**-21
periódico **131**-10
periódico estudiantil **137**-6
periodista **143**-9
perno **47**-17
perro **11**-10
perro caliente **95**-8
persianas **27**-11
pesa **35**-10, **87**-5, **123**-17
pesado(a) **69**-11
pescado **85**-9
pescador **141**-8
pescar (a pescar) **165**-10
pestillo **43**-9
petit pois **79**-13
picada **119**-13
picador **29**-17
picar **121**-24
picadura **119**-13
pie **117**-7
pie de la cama **27**-10
piel **117**-12
pierna **115**-27
pijama **103**-1
píldora **127**-16
píldoras para la gripe **127**-2
pileta **43**-19

pimentero **23**-16
pimienta **83**-5
pimiento rojo **79**-29
pimiento verde **79**-28
pimiento morron **79**-29
piña **77**-16
pinches para tender ropa **39**-19
pinta (líquida) **91**-5
pinta **91**-5, **172**
pintar **149**-2
pintarse **9**-8
pintor(a) **45**-3, **143**-4
pintura **47**-11
pinzas **47**-4
pinzas de sacar cejas **37**-10
pinzas de tender ropa **39**-19
pipa **153**-17
pique (pica) **93**-2
piquera **67**-1, **159**-28
piscina **43**-19
piso **19**-5, **21**-3
pista **133**-16
pito **157**-8
pizarra **13**-18
pizarrín **13**-19
pizarrón **13**-18
pizza **95**-10
pizzeria **61**-12
placa de matrícula **155**-11
plancha **39**-3
planchar **11**-7
planta **21**-20
plataforma **41**-14
plátano **77**-4
plata térmico **31**-20

platillo **25**-8
platito **25**-8
platito para el pan y la
   mantequillo **25**-2
plato **25**-3
plato hondo **25**-4
plato para la ensalada **25**-1
plato para la sopa **25**-4
playera **105**-1
pliego de sellos **129**-12
plomero(a) **45**-10, **143**-6
pluma **13**-5, **29**-4
pluma de agua **35**-16
plumero **143**-6
pobre **71**-16
policía **67**-10, **143**-7
pollo **85**-7
polvo **37**-14
polvo para niños **33**-1
pomada **127**-11
pompa de gasolina **155**-28
pómulo **115**-9
poncho **105**-11
ponga(n) *el proyetor* **17**-13
porche **41**-3
por ciento **50**
portabebé **31**-17, 22, 25
portacarga **151**-16
portal **41**-3
portero(a) **133**-24, **141**-4
portero automático **43**-2
portero eléctrico **43**-2
posición de trabajo **151**-8
postigo **41**-7
pote **91**-1
practicar el piano **11**-18
prefijo telefónico **3**-12
prenda(n) *el proyector*
   17-13

prendedor **107**-5
prensa de banco **47**-7
preocupado(a) **75**-6
preparar el almuerzo **9**-17
preparar el desayuno **9**-16
preparar la cena **9**-18
prima **7**-5
primavera **163**-29
primera clase **129**-5
primo **7**-5
programador(a) **141**-2
proyector de diapositivas
   13-32
proyector de películas
   13-34
proyector de transparencias
   13-32
pruebas **125**-14
pruebas de sangre **125**-15
psiquiatra **123**-14
puerco **85**-4
puerta **161**-11
puerta de atrás **41**-15
puerta de la cochera **41**-12
puerta del estacionamiento
   41-12
puerta del garaje **41**-12
puerta principal **41**-4
puesto **25**
puesto de periódicos **67**-15
pulgar **117**-3
pulmones **117**-16
pulsera **107**-7
puntos **125**-4
pupitre **13**-8

quemadura de sol **119**-14
quemarse (me quemé)
   121-19

queso **81**-6
queso crema **81**-9
quesoburguesa **95**-7
quieto(a) **71**-12
quijada **115**-10

rábano **79**-22
racimo **89**-5
radiator **155**-22
radio **157**-10
radio reloj **27**-14
radiografías **125**-13
radiólogo **123**-3
ralle(a) **93**-4
rápido(a) **69**-15
rasguñarse **121**-17
rasparse **121**-17
rastrillo **47**-21
rayos X (equis) **125**-13
rebane(a) **93**-3
recámara **27**
recepción **131**-2
receta médica **125**-1
recetas **93**
recogedor **39**-2
recoja(n) *las pruebas* **17**-10
recoja(n) *los exámenes*
   17-10
recto(a) **69**-17
redondela **35**-3
refajo **103**-11
refresquería **61**-1
refrigerador **29**-26
refrigeradora **29**-26
refugio para pobres **19**-11
regadera **35**-23
régimen **125**-8
registradora **87**-6

regla **13**-14
rejilla para la chimenea
   21-25
relámpago(s) **163**-13
relampagueando **163**-13
reloj **13**-16, **107**-6
reloj de pulsera **107**-6
reloj marcador **151**-1
remolacha **79**-30
reparador de
   electrodomésticos **45**-5
reparador de televisión
   45-6
repartidor **141**-5
repartidor de helados
   65-7
repartir *pizzas* **147**-6
repisa **13**-20, **21**-23
repollito **79**-18
repollo **79**-2
reportero(a) **143**-9
repostería **57**-1
requesón **81**-10
resfriado **119**-8
residencia estudiantil **19**-6
respirar con dificultad
   121-9
resta **50**
restaurante **53**-2
retorcerse **121**-13
retrato **21**-26
retrete **35**-2
retroproyector **13**-29
revise(n) *las respuestas*
   17-3, 9
revise(n) *sus contestaciones*
   17-3, 9

revista (literaria) **131**-11,
   137-8
revuelva(e) **93**-6, 17
rico **71**-15
riel **159**-5
riñones **117**-26
rizado(a) **69**-20
rodillo **47**-13, **115**-29
rojo **99**-1
rollo **91**-4
rollo de sellos **129**-13
romo(a) **71**-34
romperse **121**-20
ropa **100**
ropero **27**-15, **31**-3
rosa **99**-2
rosado **99**-2

sábana **27**-5
sacapuntas **13**-26
saco **101**-10
sacudir **11**-3
sal **83**-4
sala **161**-11
sala de clases **12**, **133**-6
sala de espera **161**-12
sala de profesores **133**-10
salero **23**-15
salón de belleza **59**-6
salón de clases **133**-6
salón de profesores **133**-10
salpullido **119**-12
salsa china **83**-8
salsa de soya **83**-8
salsa de tomate **83**-2
saltée (saltéa) **93**-8, 19
sandalias **103**-18
sandía **77**-17

The bold number indicates the page(s) on which the word appears; the number that follows indicates the word's location in the illustration and in the word list on the page. For example, "apple **77**-1" indicates that the word *apple* is on page 77 and is item number 1.